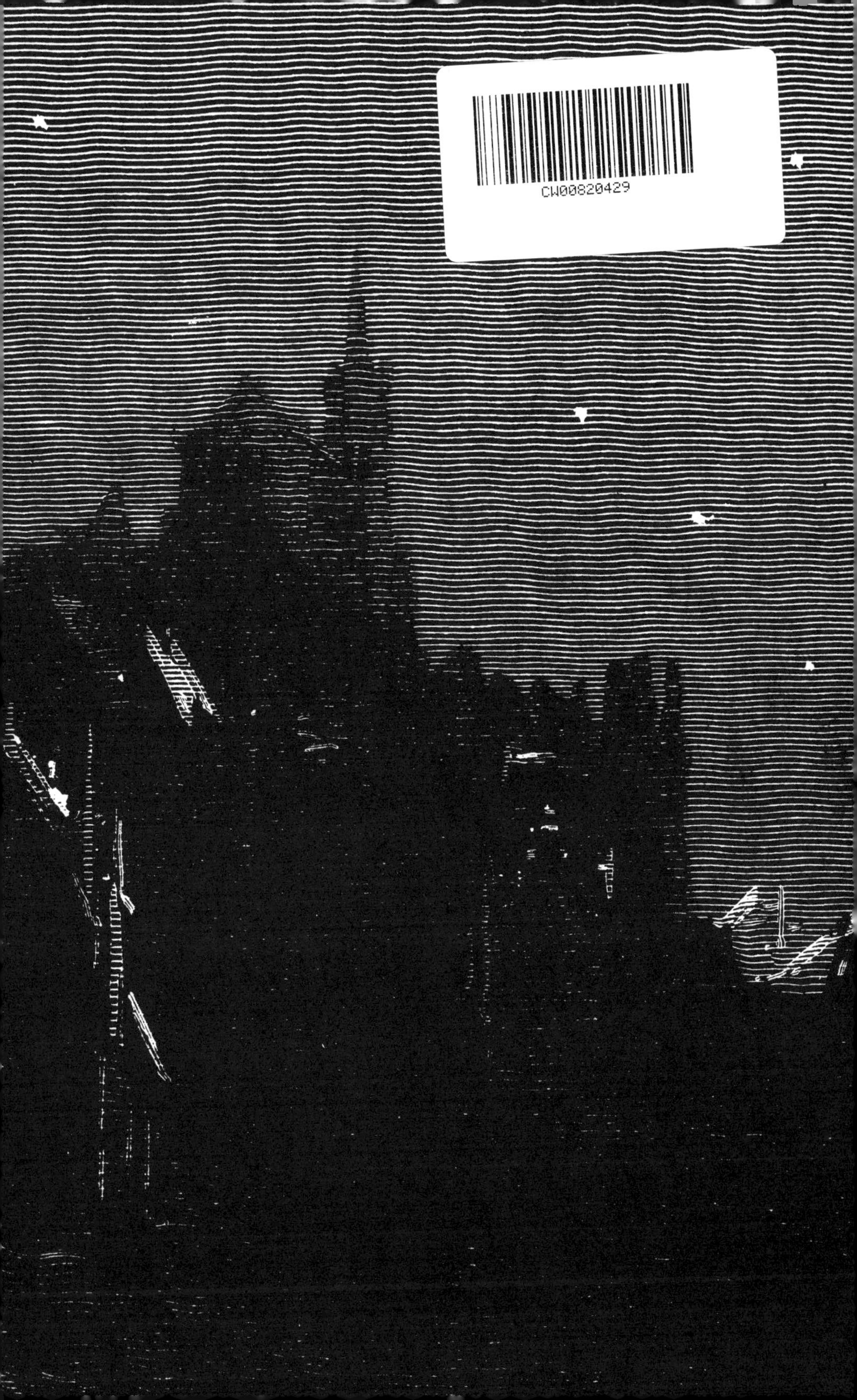

The Dark Horse Book of
Hauntings

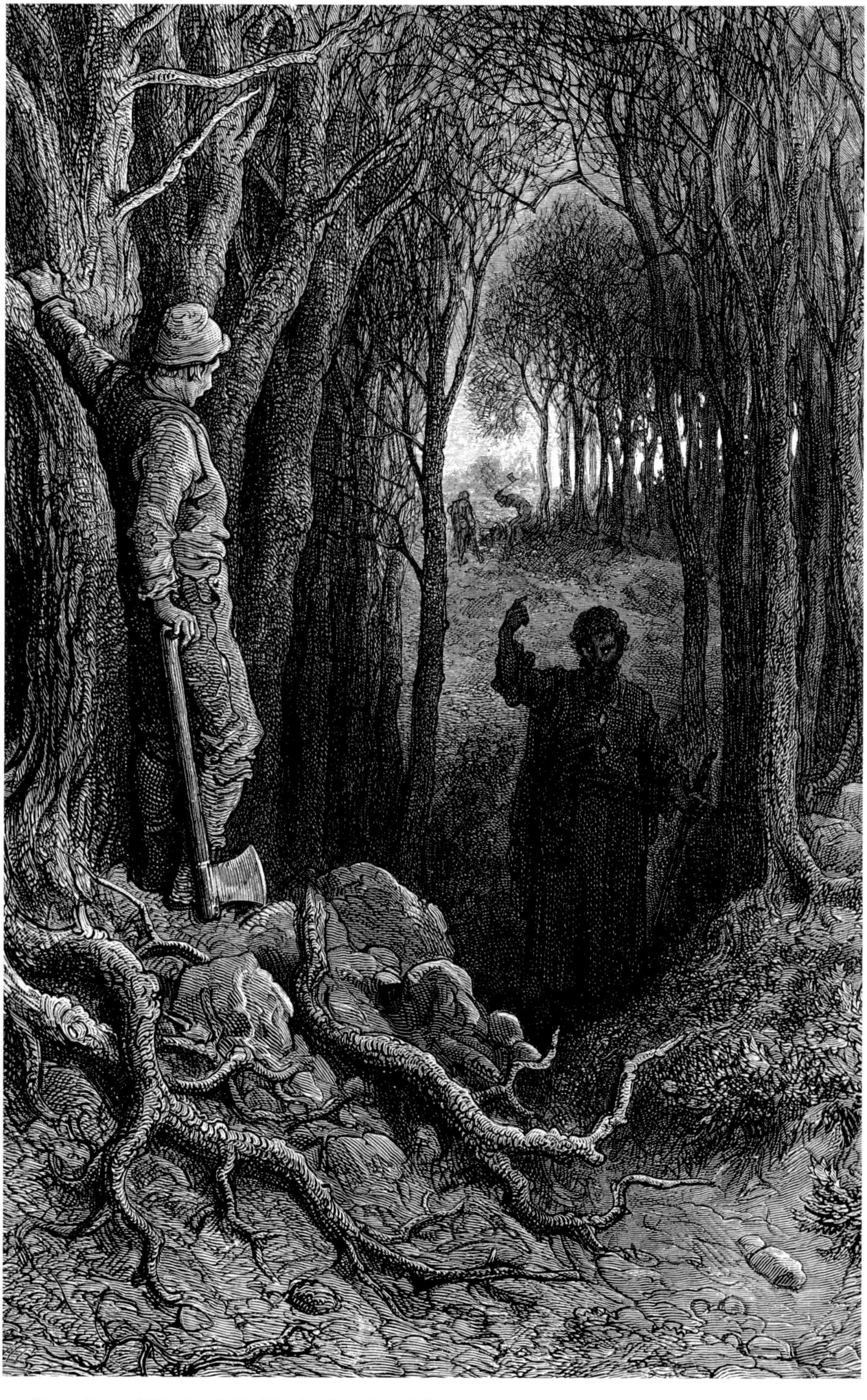

From Samuel Taylor Coleridge's *The Rime of the Ancient Mariner*, illustrated by Gustave Doré.

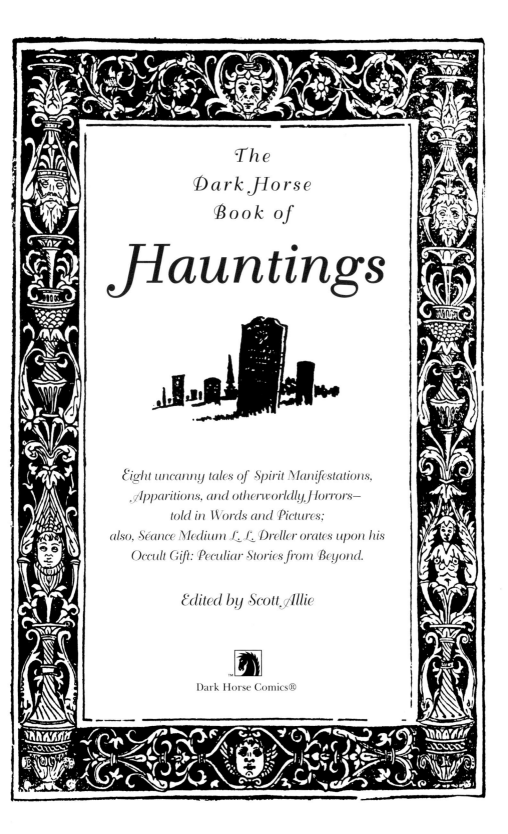

The
Dark Horse
Book of

Hauntings

Eight uncanny tales of Spirit Manifestations,
Apparitions, and otherworldly Horrors—
told in Words and Pictures;
also, Séance Medium L. L. Dreller orates upon his
Occult Gift: Peculiar Stories from Beyond.

Edited by Scott Allie

Dark Horse Comics®

Cover Illustration
Gary Gianni

Cover Design and Colors
Jim Keegan

Assistant Editor
Matt Dryer

Associate Editor
Shawna Ervin-Gore

Art Director
Mark Cox

Designers
Mark Cox
David Nestelle
Lia Ribacchi
Lani Schreibstein

Publisher
Mike Richardson

Published by
Dark Horse Comics, Inc.
10956 SE Main Street
Milwaukie, OR 97222

First edition
August 2003
ISBN: 1-56971-958-6

1 3 5 7 9 10 8 6 4 2
Printed in China

Table of Contents

For Hans Holzer, Edward Gorey,
and the Fox Sisters.

Introduction

The only ghost sighting I can claim would've worked as an episode of *Scooby Doo*.

My childhood bedroom in Emerson Park in Peabody, Massachusetts was an irregularly shaped room. The ceiling sloped in because of the dormers around the windows, casting weird shadows up and down the walls. This was tempered a bit by the mural of Huey, Louie, and Dewey that my mother painted, sledding down the incline of the ceiling. There were chunks missing in the plaster above my headboard, out of which I sometimes imagined eyes peering down at me. I was fairly high-strung even as a five year old. I had lots of visions in my head of spectres and ghouls, awful-looking things that I'm still trying to work into comics.

The ghost I saw, however, was the typical childhood version of a ghost, an indistinct shape under a white sheet, floating at my window. I couldn't tell for sure if it was on the ledge outside my window or inside the room. It didn't move much, but it also didn't have a definite solidity, seemed only tentatively there. I was scared out of my mind.

The ghost disappeared, and I mellowed out, and I suppose I eventually fell asleep. In the morning, I told my mother about it. In the afternoon, I told my friends at Center School. When I got home, I told my older friends in the neighborhood, Kevin Meyers and Christine Silk. It was all I could talk about for a couple days.

When the weekend rolled around, Kevin Meyers came over, all hangdog. My mother stood by him watching the expression on my face as he explained that he and his brother had brought home a projector and a slide presentation of "A Christmas Carol"—the greatest ghost story of all time. They must have accidentally aimed it out their window, and at mine. This was what I saw. My mother thanked Kevin, and sent him home.

Over the years, I grew suspicious of the explanation. It was too convenient. Did my mother put Kevin up to it? Why didn't I ask to see the slide projector— I played with Kevin and his brother day in and day out, and there was never a projector of any kind. Not to say the ghost was real, or even that I was awake.

I've loved anthologies for as long as I can remember, and every so often my publisher, Mike Richardson, lets me do one, like the one you hold in your hands. Thanks to Mignola for narrowing down the focus of the book—he offered me a thirteen-page *Hellboy* story; I said, "Well, that's kind of a haunted -house story, so there's our theme." Thanks to Stradley for convincing me to make it a little broader, which allowed me to include his very enigmatic story, as well as German artist Uli Oesterle's "Forever." Of course, Evan Dorkin and Jill Thompson have really pushed the edges of our theme with their tale, but I don't want to give anything away about that—assuming you're the type to read the intro before the much better material inside.

If so, I suggest reading from the beginning. "Gone" takes you into the world of hauntings, and each feature takes you a little deeper, hopefully offering many surprises along the way.

BOO!

Scott Allie

Portland, Oregon

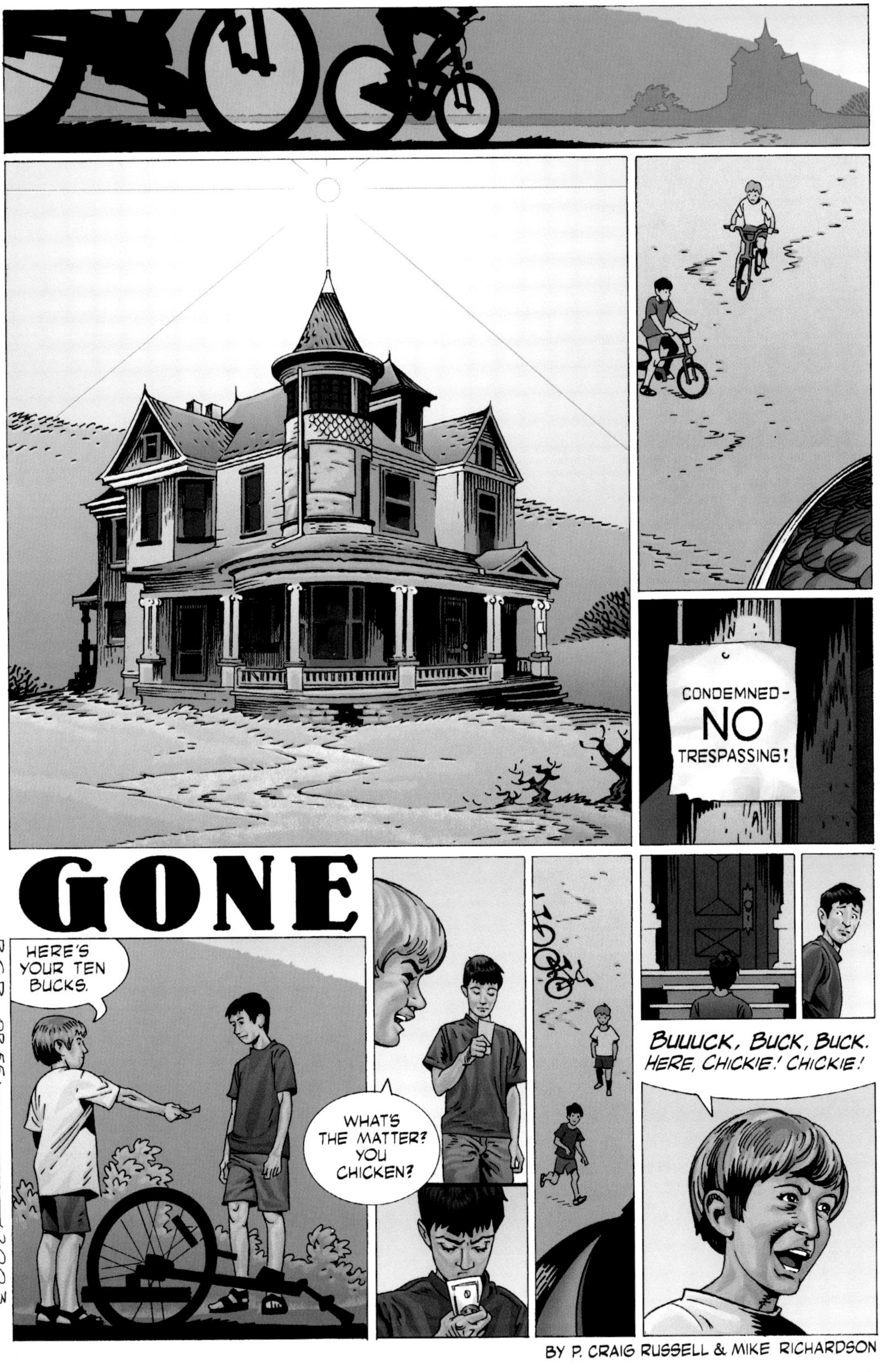
CONDEMNED -
NO
TRESPASSING!
GONE
HERE'S YOUR TEN BUCKS.
WHAT'S THE MATTER? YOU CHICKEN?
BUUUCK, BUCK, BUCK.
HERE, CHICKIE! CHICKIE!

BY P. CRAIG RUSSELL & MIKE RICHARDSON

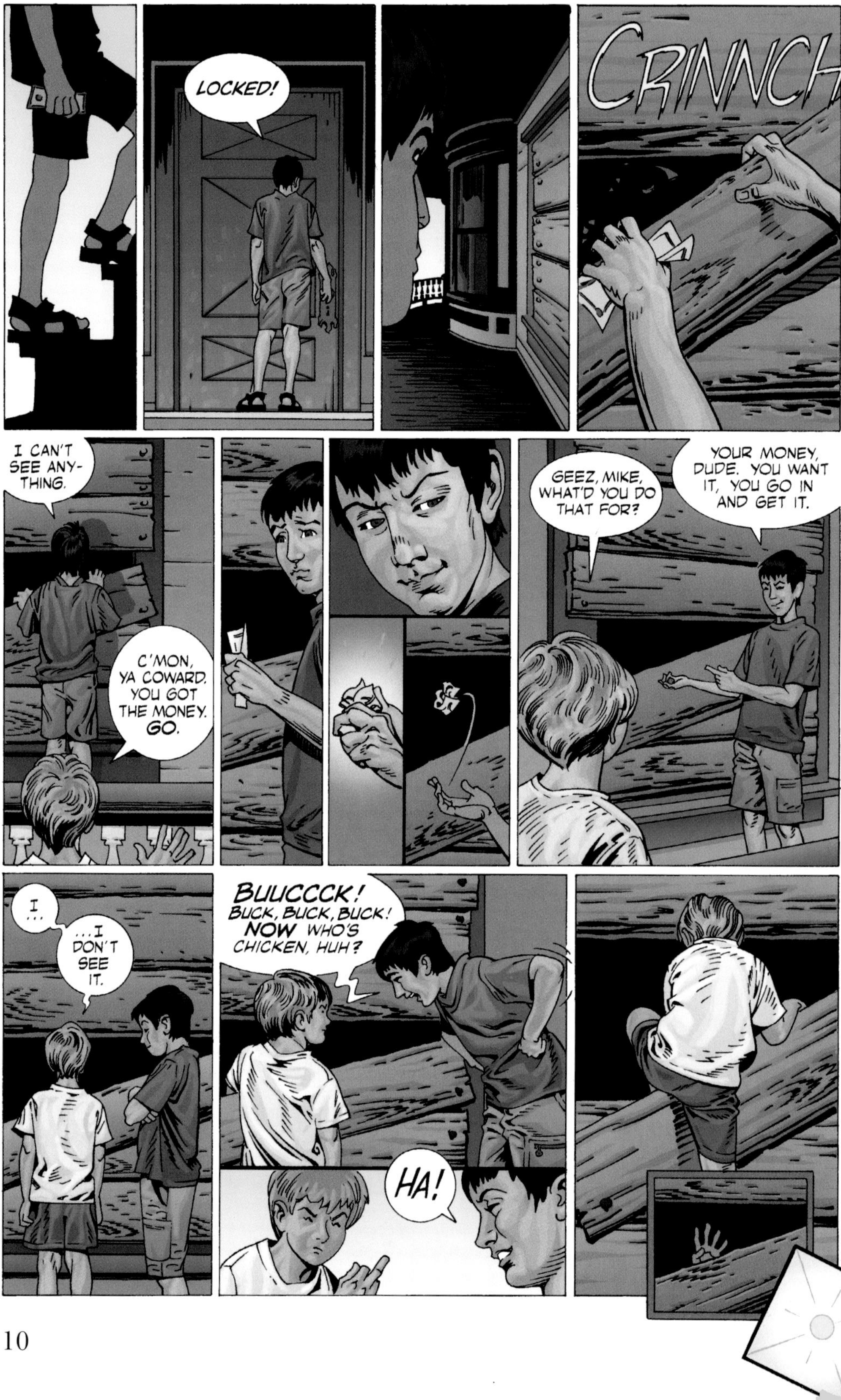
LOCKED!
CRINNCH
I CAN'T SEE ANY-THING.
C'MON, YA COWARD. YOU GOT THE MONEY. GO.
GEEZ, MIKE, WHAT'D YOU DO THAT FOR?
YOUR MONEY, DUDE. YOU WANT IT, YOU GO IN AND GET IT.
I . . .
. . . I DON'T SEE IT.
BUUCCCK! BUCK, BUCK, BUCK! NOW WHO'S CHICKEN, HUH?
HA!

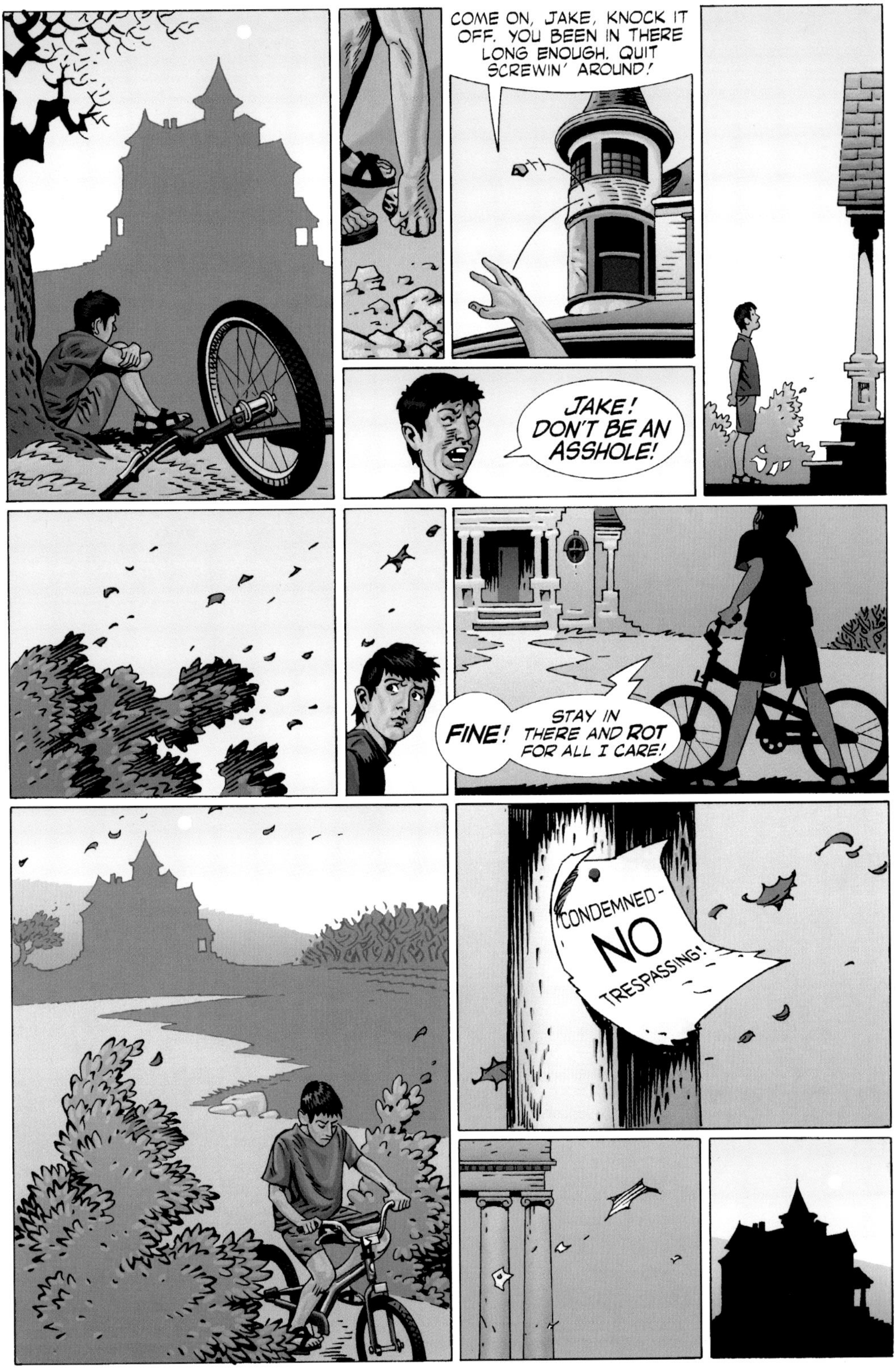
COME ON, JAKE, KNOCK IT OFF. YOU BEEN IN THERE LONG ENOUGH. QUIT SCREWIN' AROUND!
JAKE! DON'T BE AN ASSHOLE!
FINE!
STAY IN THERE AND ROT FOR ALL I CARE!
CONDEMNED- NO TRESPASSING!

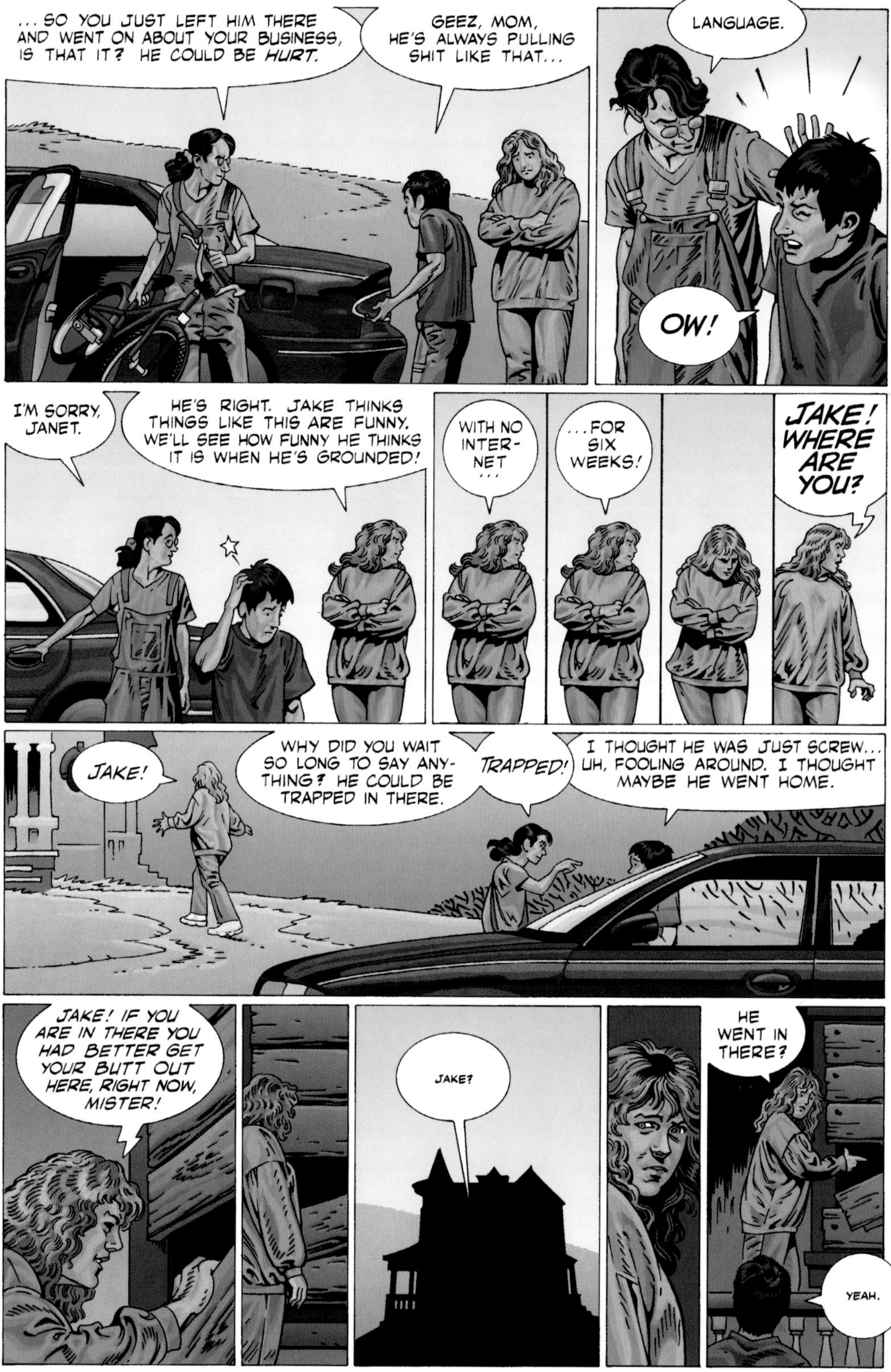
...SO YOU JUST LEFT HIM THERE AND WENT ON ABOUT YOUR BUSINESS, IS THAT IT? HE COULD BE HURT.
GEEZ, MOM, HE'S ALWAYS PULLING SHIT LIKE THAT...
LANGUAGE.
OW!
I'M SORRY, JANET.
HE'S RIGHT. JAKE THINKS THINGS LIKE THIS ARE FUNNY. WE'LL SEE HOW FUNNY HE THINKS IT IS WHEN HE'S GROUNDED!
WITH NO INTER-NET...
...FOR SIX WEEKS!
JAKE! WHERE ARE YOU?
JAKE!
WHY DID YOU WAIT SO LONG TO SAY ANY-THING? HE COULD BE TRAPPED IN THERE.
TRAPPED!
I THOUGHT HE WAS JUST SCREW... UH, FOOLING AROUND. I THOUGHT MAYBE HE WENT HOME.
JAKE! IF YOU ARE IN THERE YOU HAD BETTER GET YOUR BUTT OUT HERE, RIGHT NOW, MISTER!
JAKE?
HE WENT IN THERE?
YEAH.

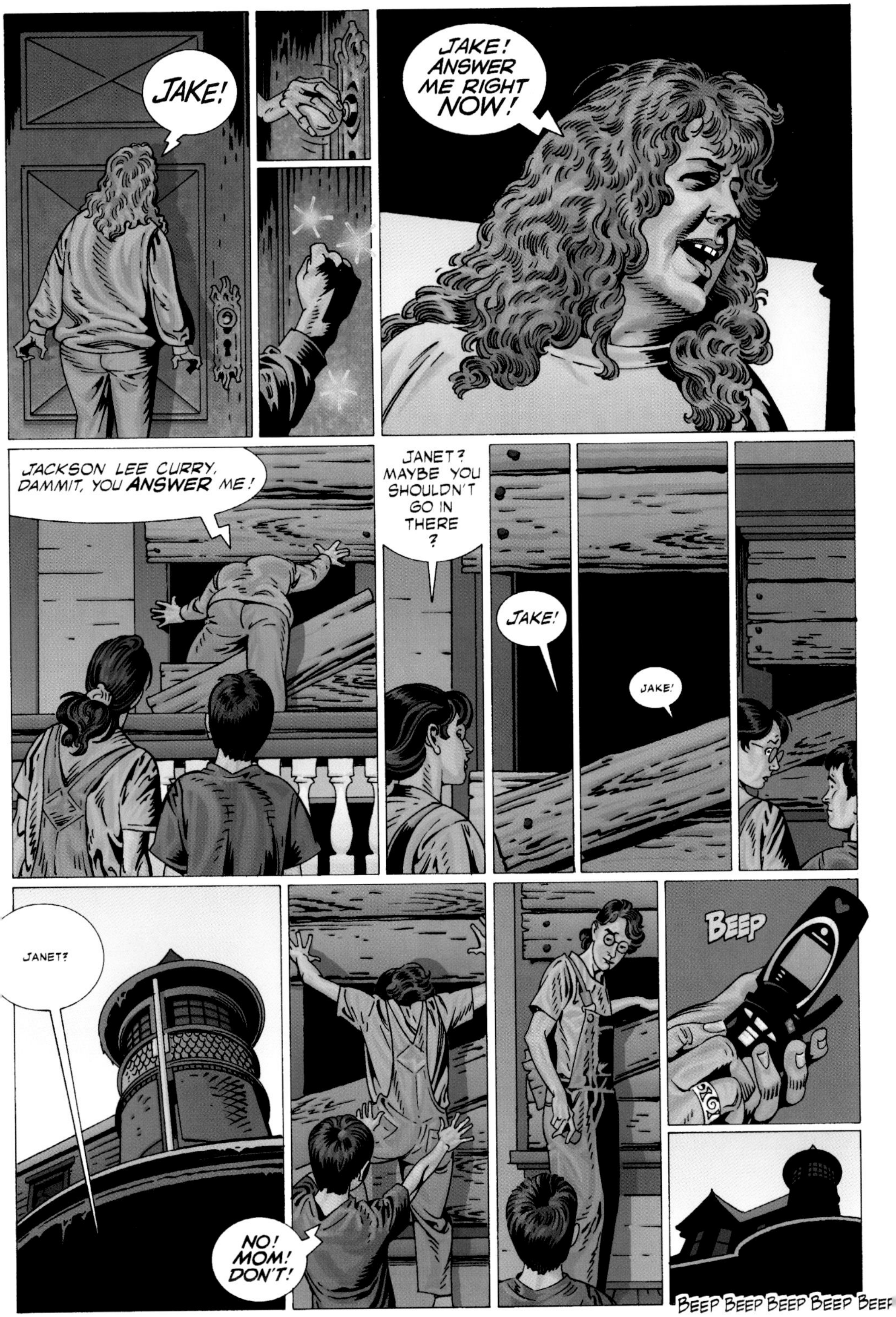
JAKE!
JAKE! ANSWER ME RIGHT NOW!
JACKSON LEE CURRY, DAMMIT, YOU ANSWER ME!
JANET? MAYBE YOU SHOULDN'T GO IN THERE?
JAKE!
JAKE!
JANET?
NO! MOM! DON'T!
BEEP
BEEP BEEP BEEP BEEP BEEP

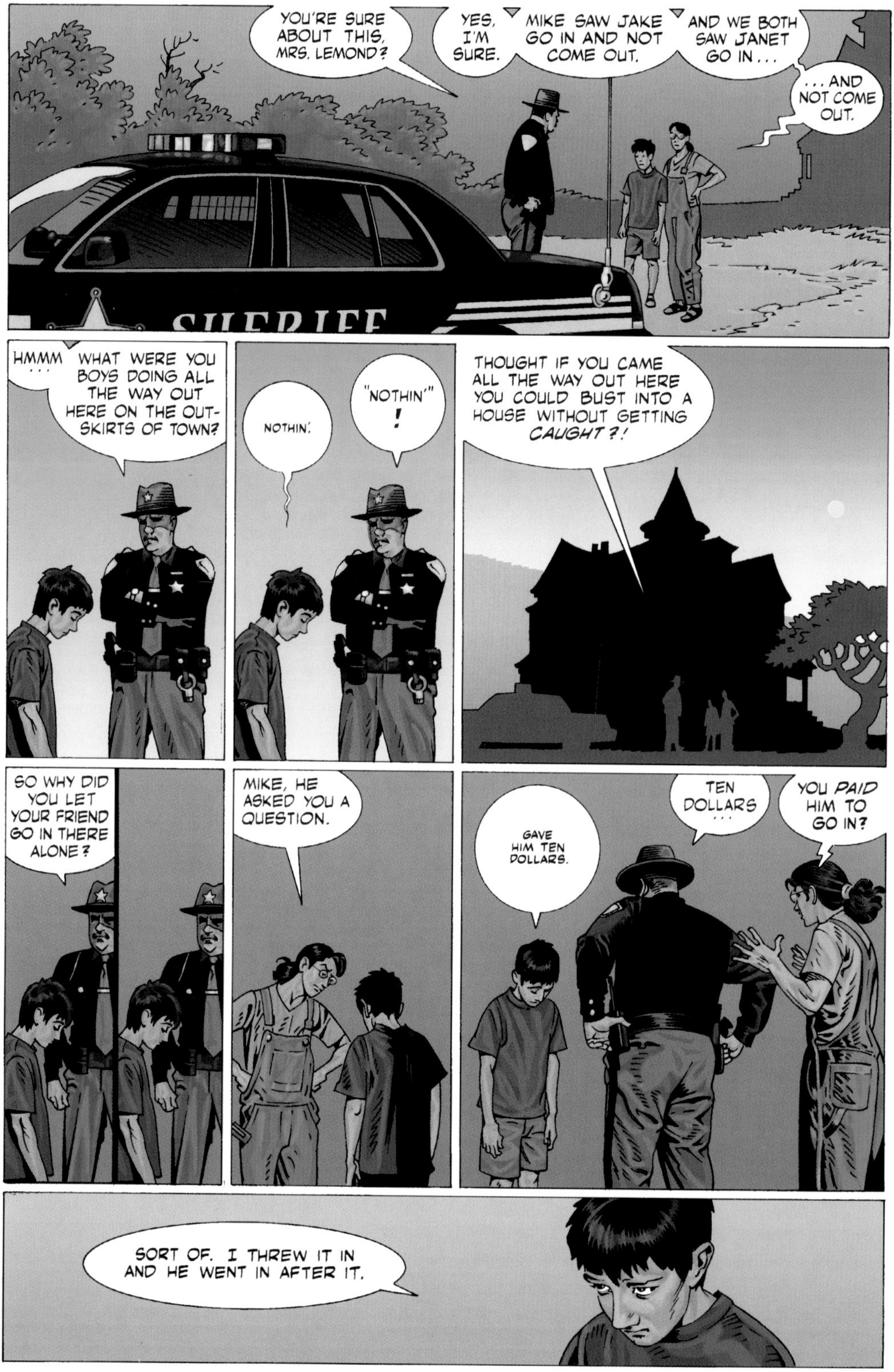
YOU'RE SURE ABOUT THIS, MRS. LEMOND?
YES, I'M SURE.
MIKE SAW JAKE GO IN AND NOT COME OUT.
AND WE BOTH SAW JANET GO IN...
...AND NOT COME OUT.
SHERIFF
HMMM...
WHAT WERE YOU BOYS DOING ALL THE WAY OUT HERE ON THE OUTSKIRTS OF TOWN?
NOTHIN'.
"NOTHIN'"!
THOUGHT IF YOU CAME ALL THE WAY OUT HERE YOU COULD BUST INTO A HOUSE WITHOUT GETTING CAUGHT?!
SO WHY DID YOU LET YOUR FRIEND GO IN THERE ALONE?
MIKE, HE ASKED YOU A QUESTION.
GAVE HIM TEN DOLLARS.
TEN DOLLARS...
YOU PAID HIM TO GO IN?
SORT OF. I THREW IT IN AND HE WENT IN AFTER IT.

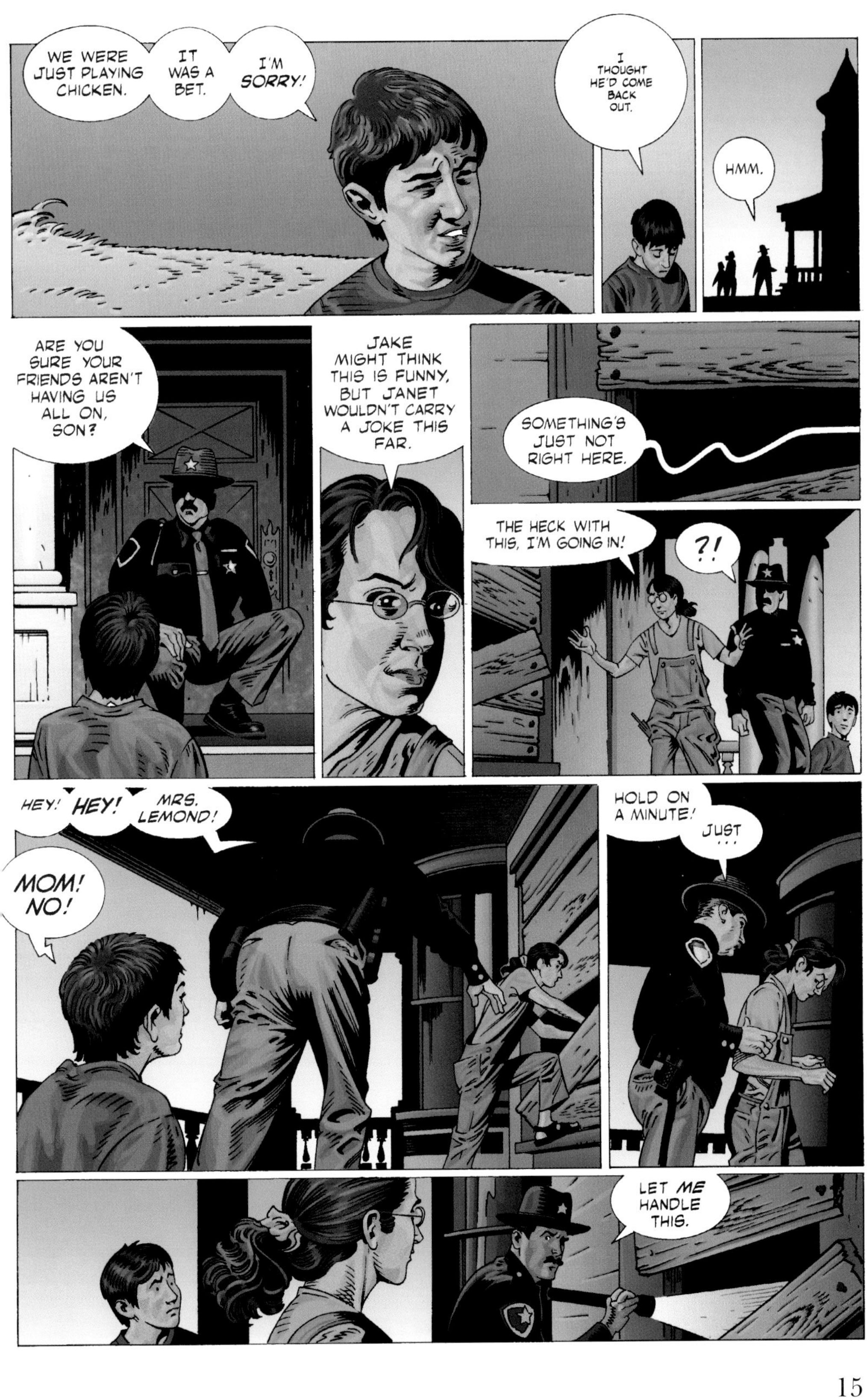
WE WERE JUST PLAYING CHICKEN.
IT WAS A BET.
I'M *SORRY!*
I THOUGHT HE'D COME BACK OUT.
HMM.
ARE YOU SURE YOUR FRIENDS AREN'T HAVING US ALL ON, SON?
JAKE MIGHT THINK THIS IS FUNNY, BUT JANET WOULDN'T CARRY A JOKE THIS FAR.
SOMETHING'S JUST NOT RIGHT HERE.
THE HECK WITH THIS, I'M GOING IN!
?!
HEY!
HEY!
MRS. LEMOND!
MOM! NO!
HOLD ON A MINUTE!
JUST . . .
LET *ME* HANDLE THIS.

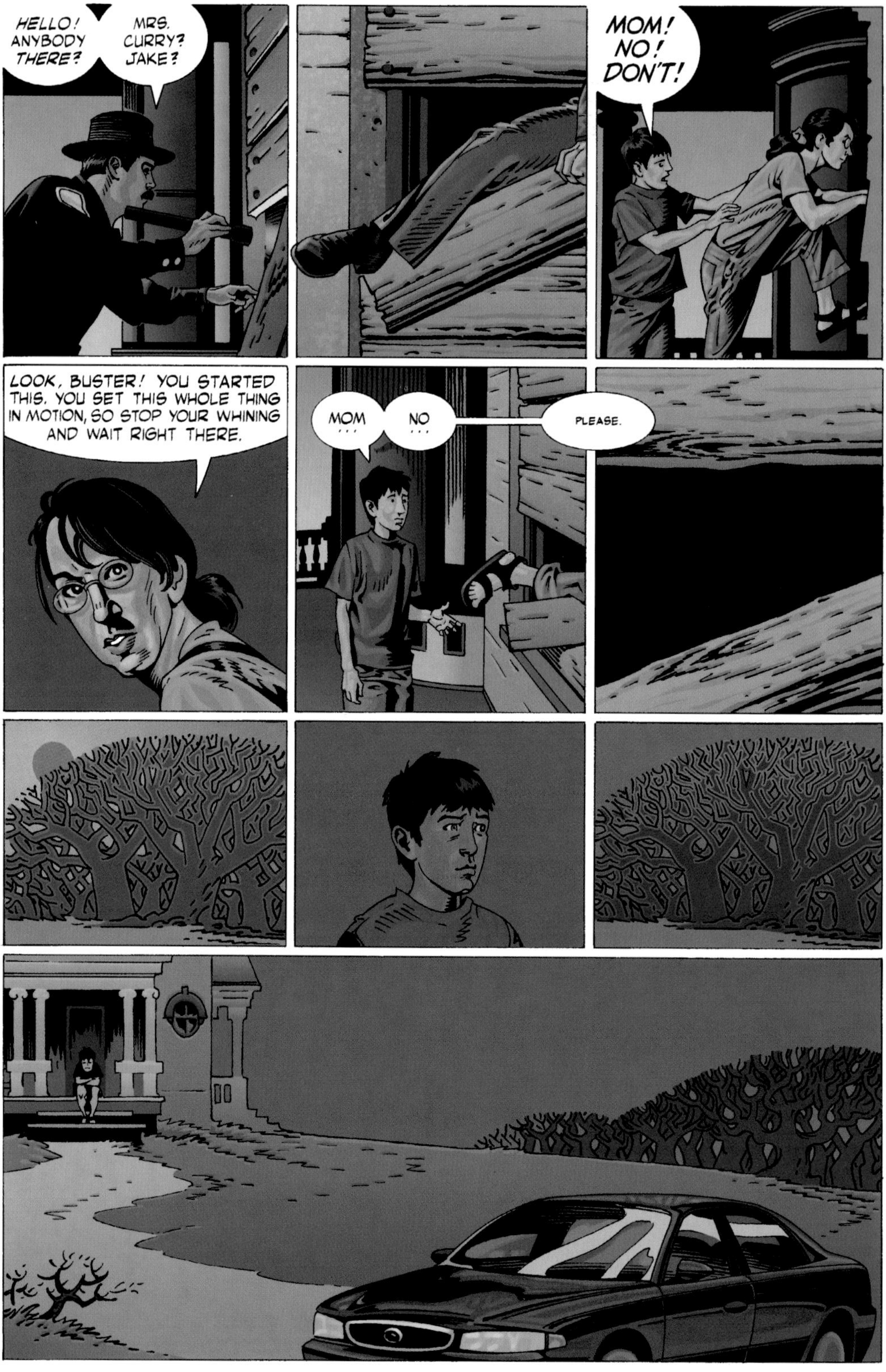
HELLO! ANYBODY THERE?
MRS. CURRY? JAKE?
MOM! NO! DON'T!
LOOK, BUSTER! YOU STARTED THIS. YOU SET THIS WHOLE THING IN MOTION, SO STOP YOUR WHINING AND WAIT RIGHT THERE.
MOM ...
NO ...
PLEASE.

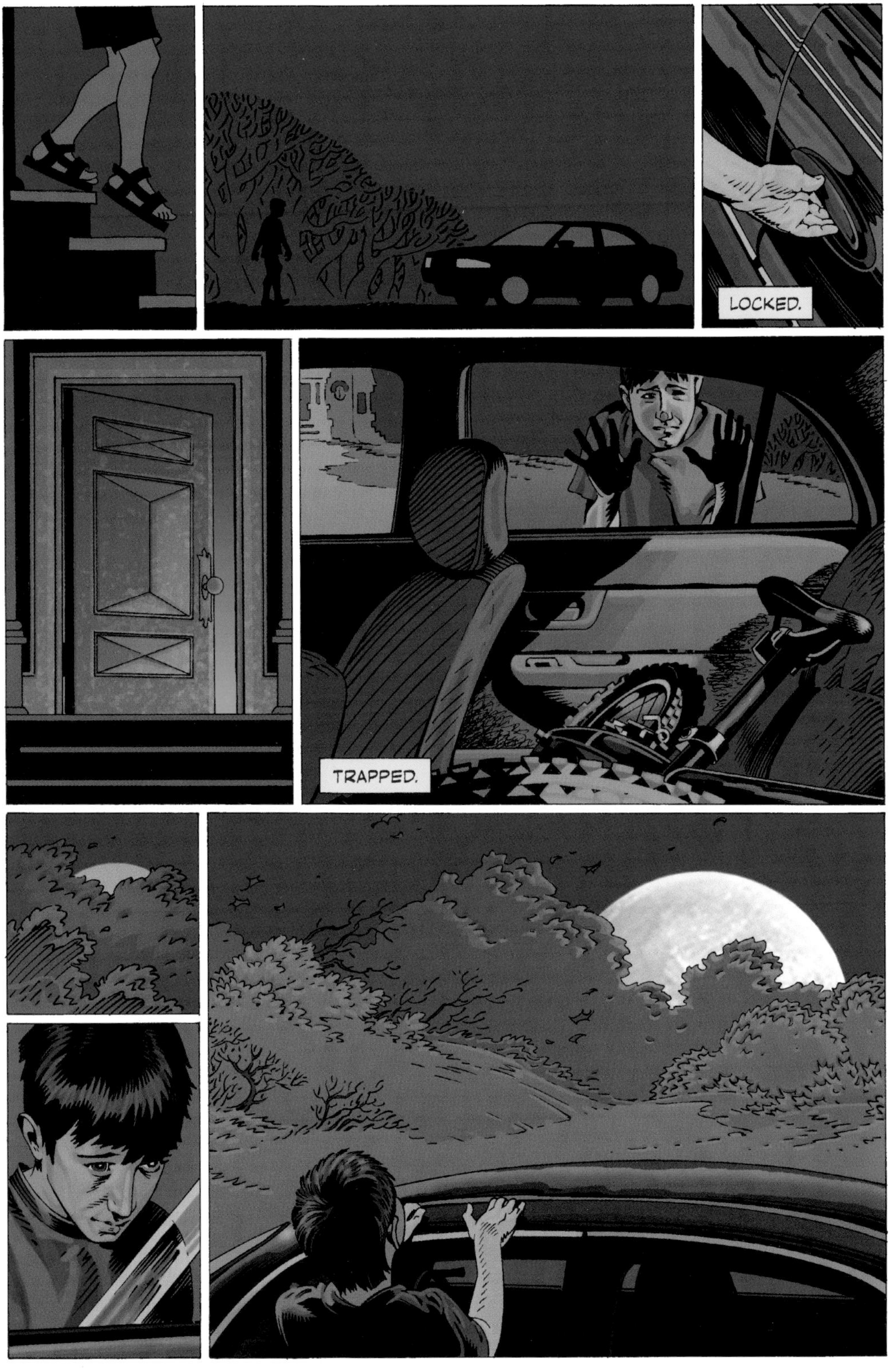
LOCKED.
TRAPPED.

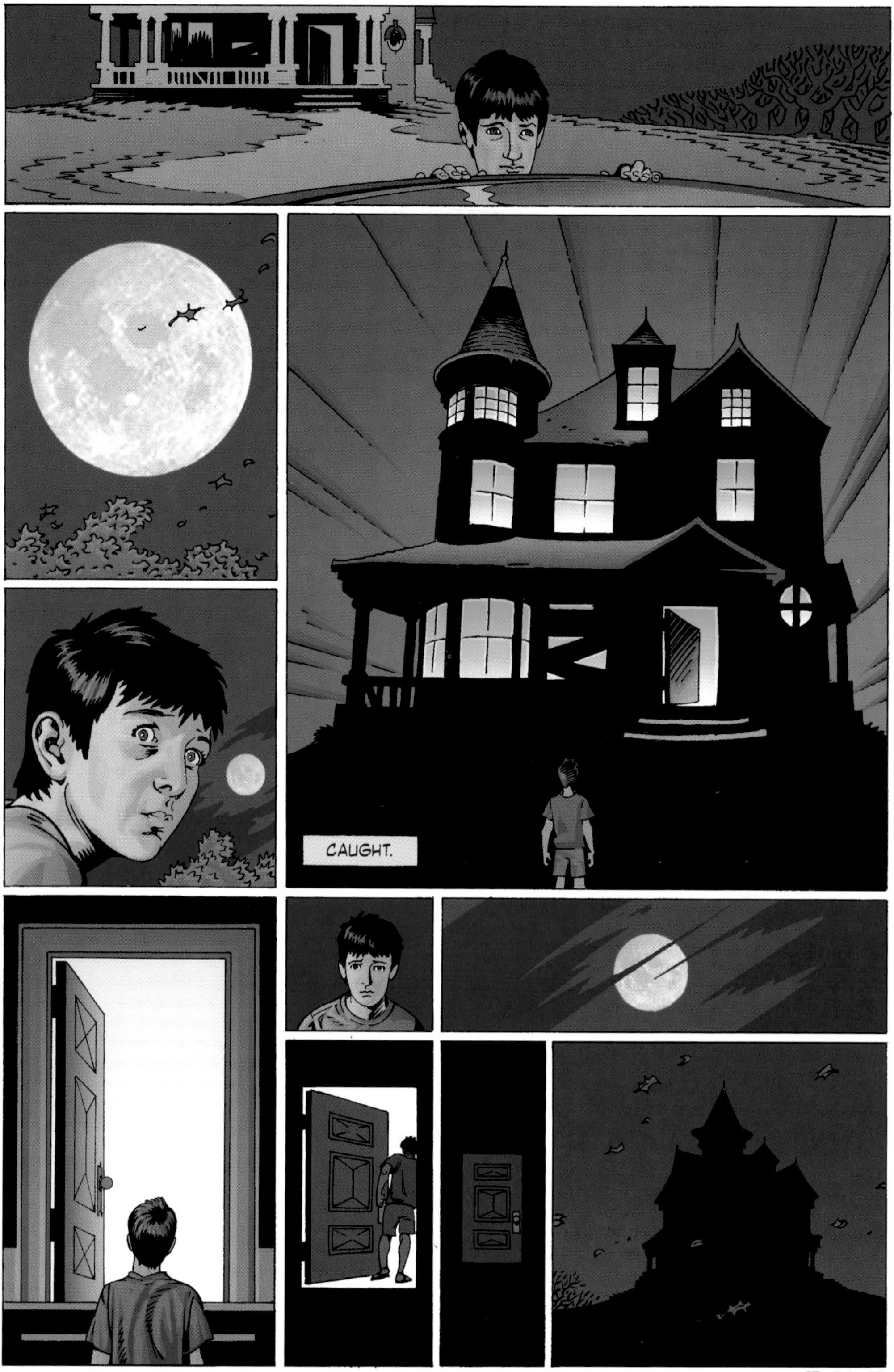
CAUGHT.

END

Dr. Carp's Experiment

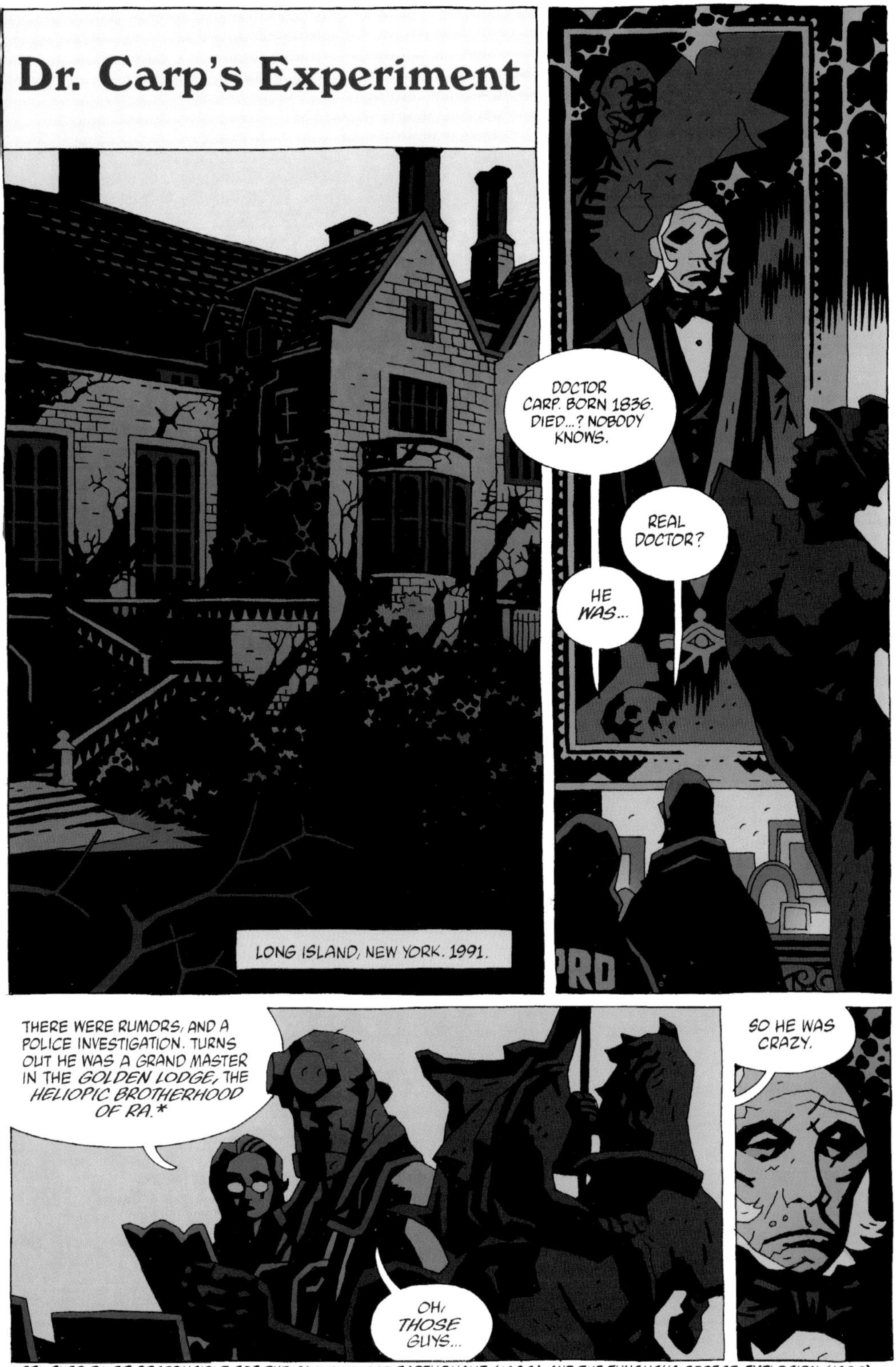
LONG ISLAND, NEW YORK. 1991.
DOCTOR CARP. BORN 1836. DIED...? NOBODY KNOWS.
REAL DOCTOR?
HE *WAS*...
THERE WERE RUMORS, AND A POLICE INVESTIGATION. TURNS OUT HE WAS A GRAND MASTER IN THE *GOLDEN LODGE*, THE *HELIOPIC BROTHERHOOD OF RA*.*
OH, *THOSE* GUYS...
SO HE WAS CRAZY.

**BELIEVED TO BE RESPONSIBLE FOR THE SAN FRANCISCO EARTHQUAKE (1906) AND THE TUNGUSKA FOREST EXPLOSION (1908).*

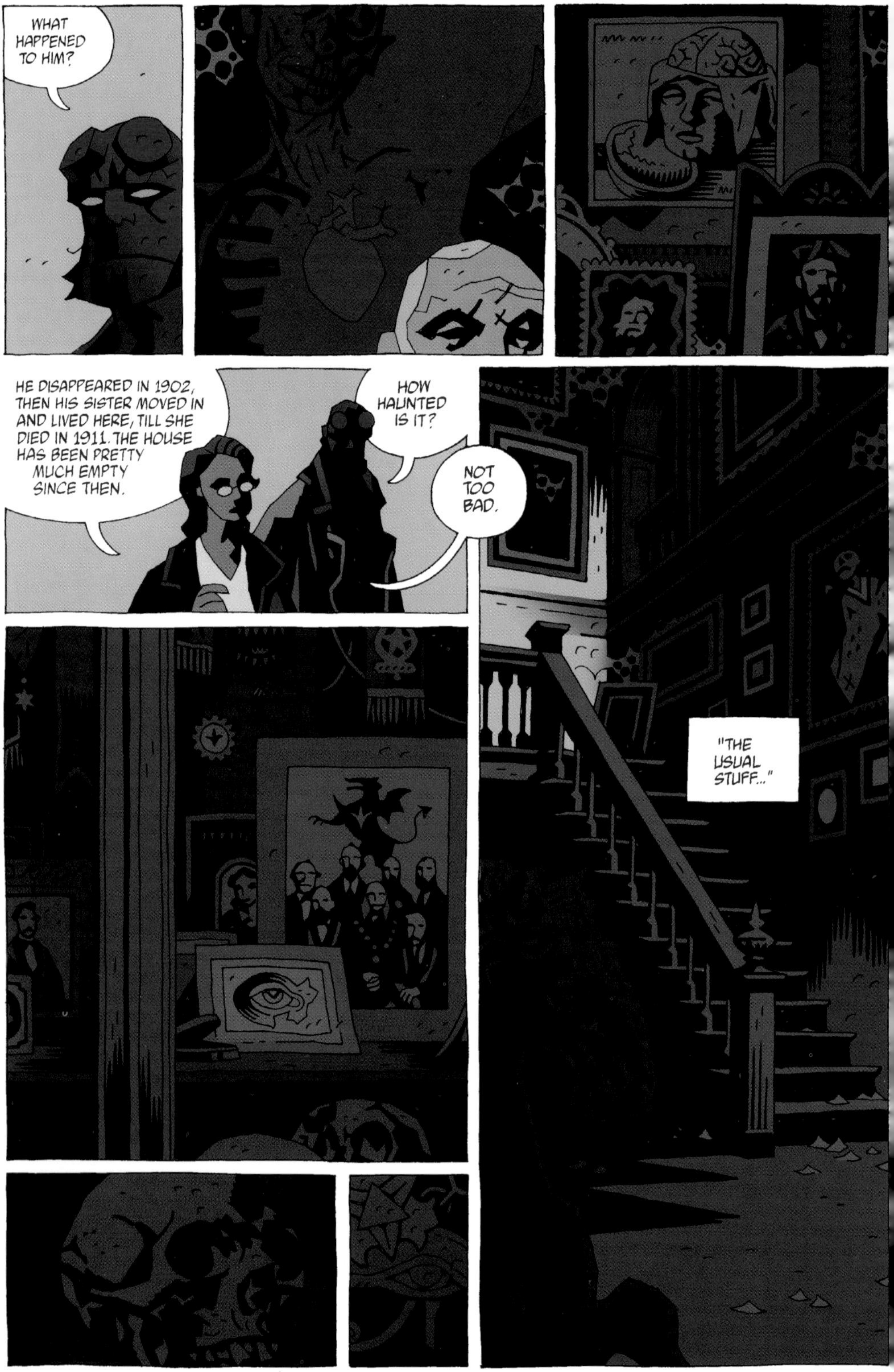
WHAT HAPPENED TO HIM?
HE DISAPPEARED IN 1902, THEN HIS SISTER MOVED IN AND LIVED HERE, TILL SHE DIED IN 1911. THE HOUSE HAS BEEN PRETTY MUCH EMPTY SINCE THEN.
HOW HAUNTED IS IT?
NOT TOO BAD.
"THE USUAL STUFF..."

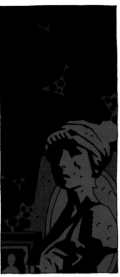

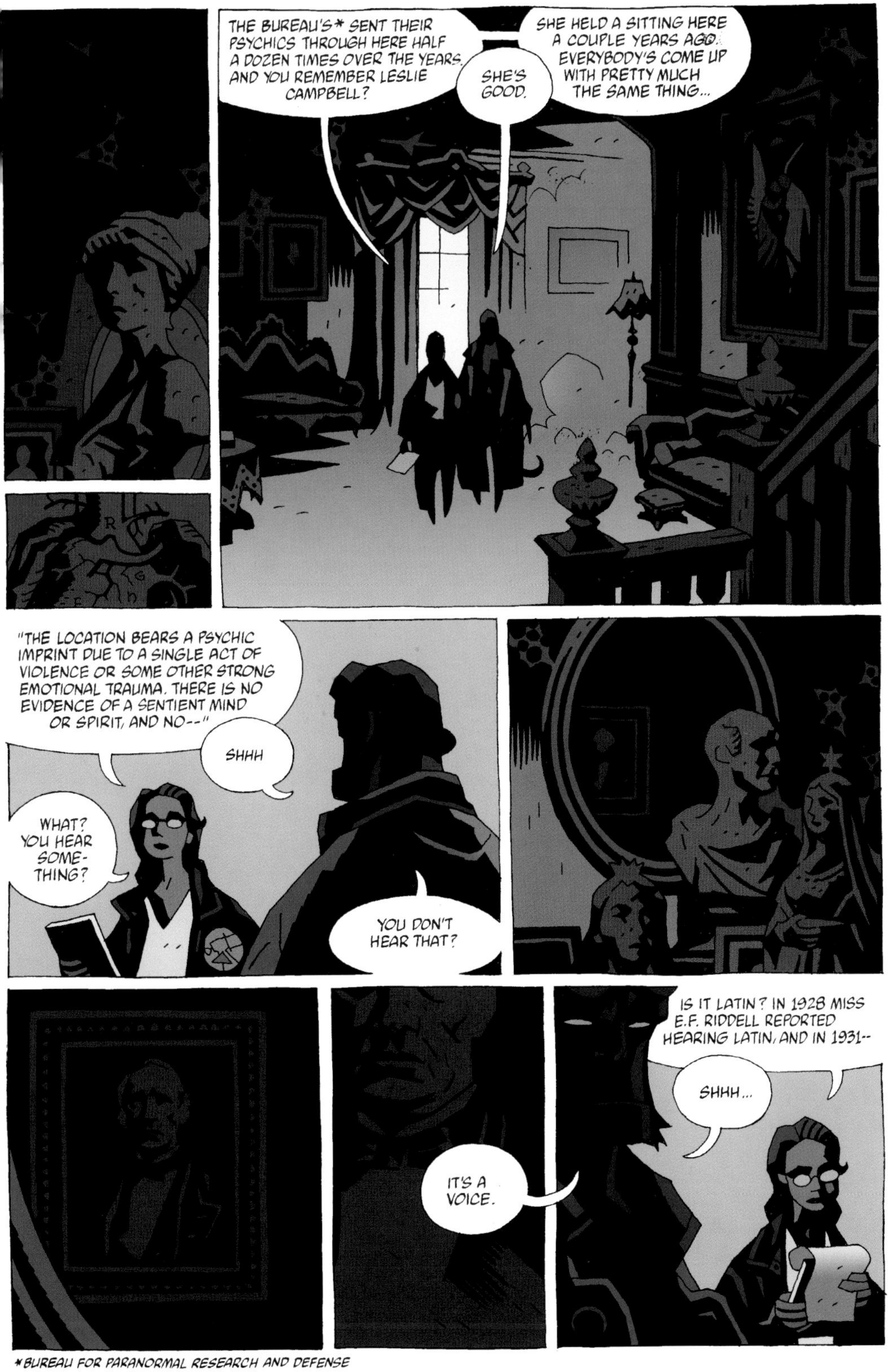
THE BUREAU'S* SENT THEIR PSYCHICS THROUGH HERE HALF A DOZEN TIMES OVER THE YEARS. AND YOU REMEMBER LESLIE CAMPBELL?
SHE'S GOOD.
SHE HELD A SITTING HERE A COUPLE YEARS AGO. EVERYBODY'S COME UP WITH PRETTY MUCH THE SAME THING...
"THE LOCATION BEARS A PSYCHIC IMPRINT DUE TO A SINGLE ACT OF VIOLENCE OR SOME OTHER STRONG EMOTIONAL TRAUMA. THERE IS NO EVIDENCE OF A SENTIENT MIND OR SPIRIT, AND NO--"
SHHH
WHAT? YOU HEAR SOME-THING?
YOU DON'T HEAR THAT?
IS IT LATIN? IN 1928 MISS E.F. RIDDELL REPORTED HEARING LATIN, AND IN 1931--
SHHH...
IT'S A VOICE.

*BUREAU FOR PARANORMAL RESEARCH AND DEFENSE

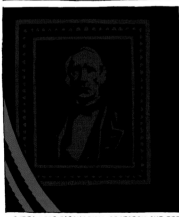

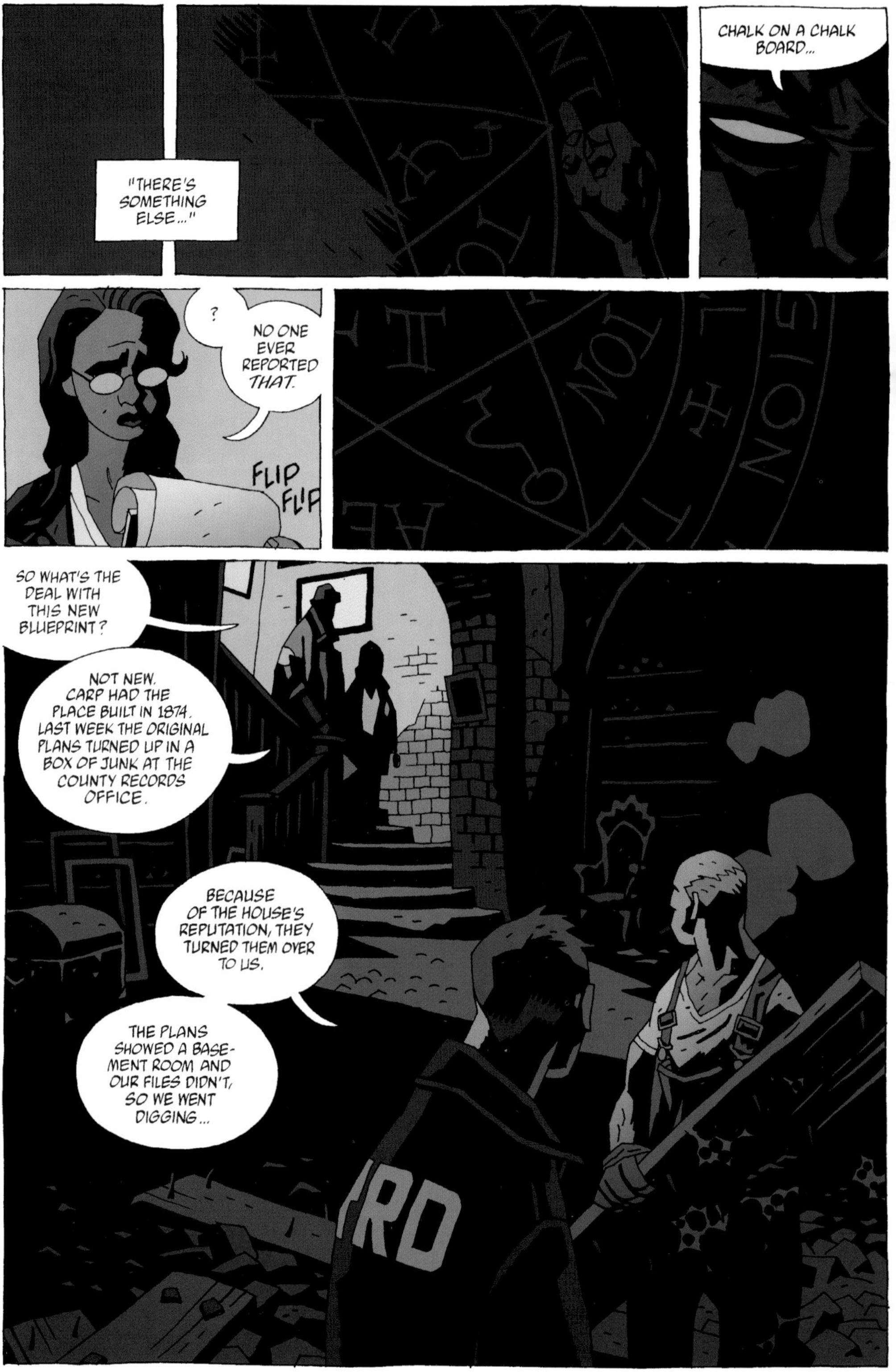

"THERE'S SOMETHING ELSE..."
CHALK ON A CHALK BOARD...
?
NO ONE EVER REPORTED *THAT.*
FLIP FLIP
SO WHAT'S THE DEAL WITH THIS NEW BLUEPRINT?
NOT NEW. CARP HAD THE PLACE BUILT IN 1874. LAST WEEK THE ORIGINAL PLANS TURNED UP IN A BOX OF JUNK AT THE COUNTY RECORDS OFFICE.
BECAUSE OF THE HOUSE'S REPUTATION, THEY TURNED THEM OVER TO US.
THE PLANS SHOWED A BASE-MENT ROOM AND OUR FILES DIDN'T, SO WE WENT DIGGING...

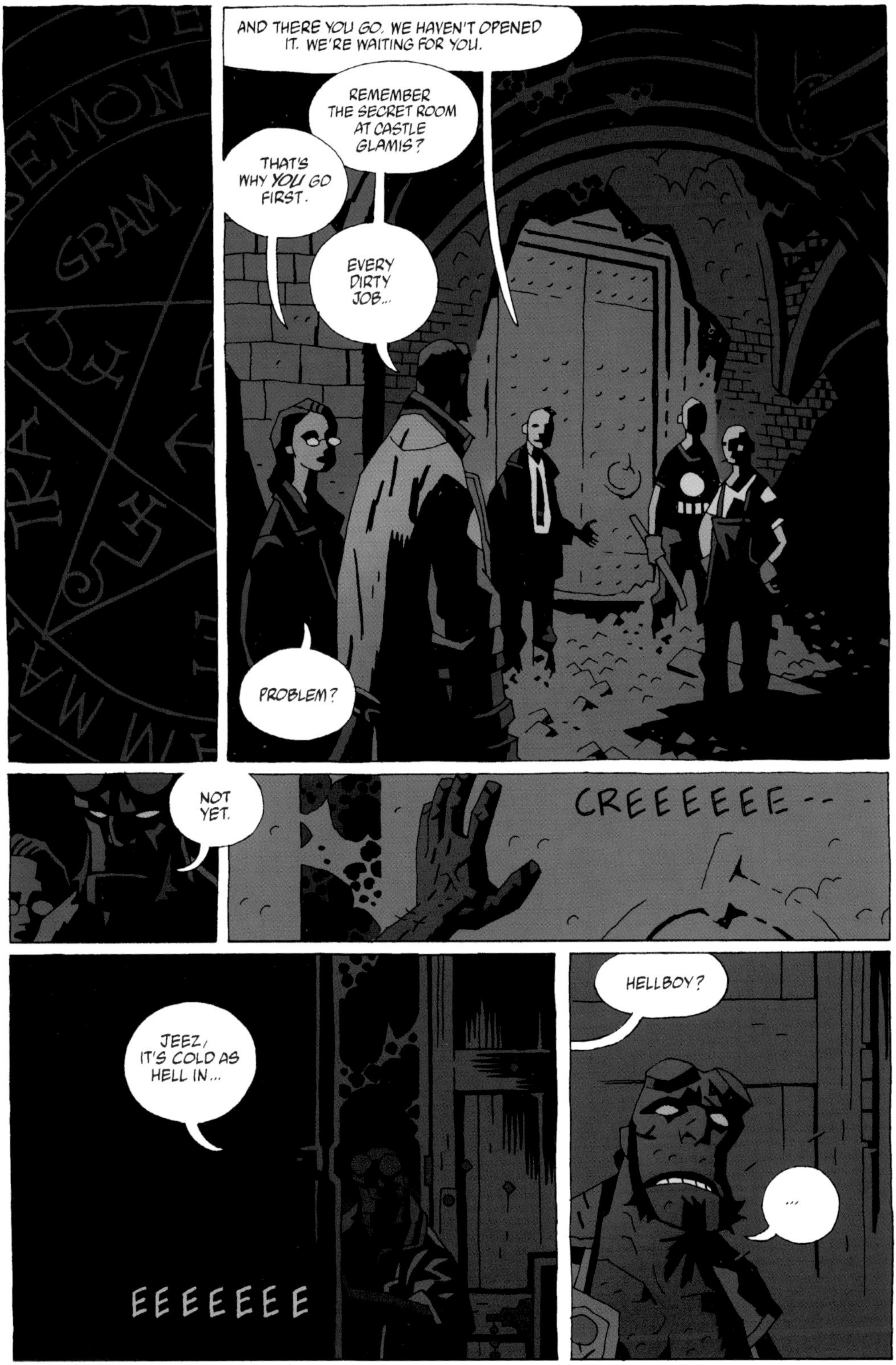
AND THERE YOU GO. WE HAVEN'T OPENED IT. WE'RE WAITING FOR YOU.
REMEMBER THE SECRET ROOM AT CASTLE GLAMIS?
THAT'S WHY YOU GO FIRST.
EVERY DIRTY JOB...
PROBLEM?
NOT YET.
CREEEEEEE---
JEEZ, IT'S COLD AS HELL IN...
EEEEEEE
HELLBOY?
...

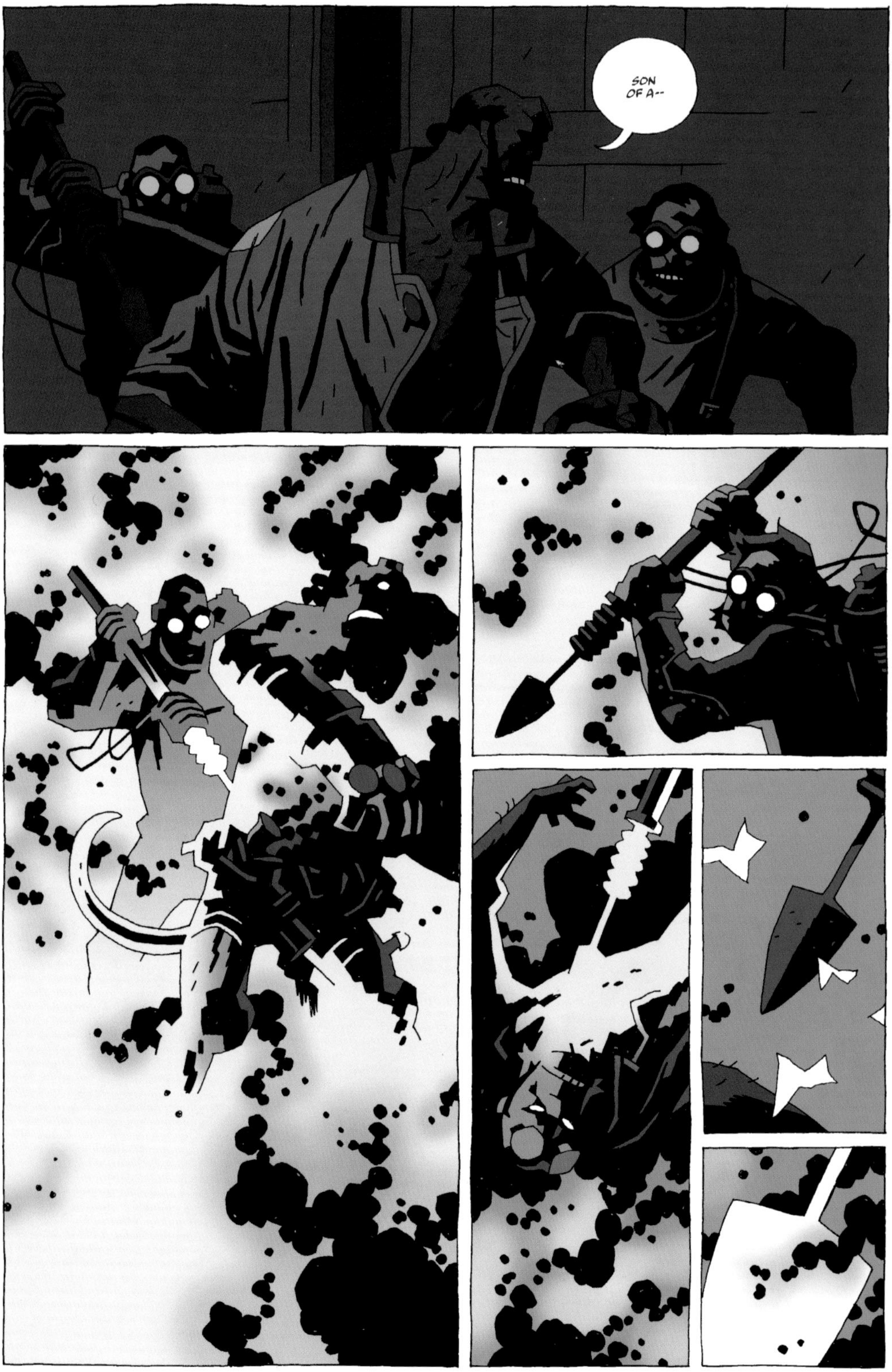
SON OF A--

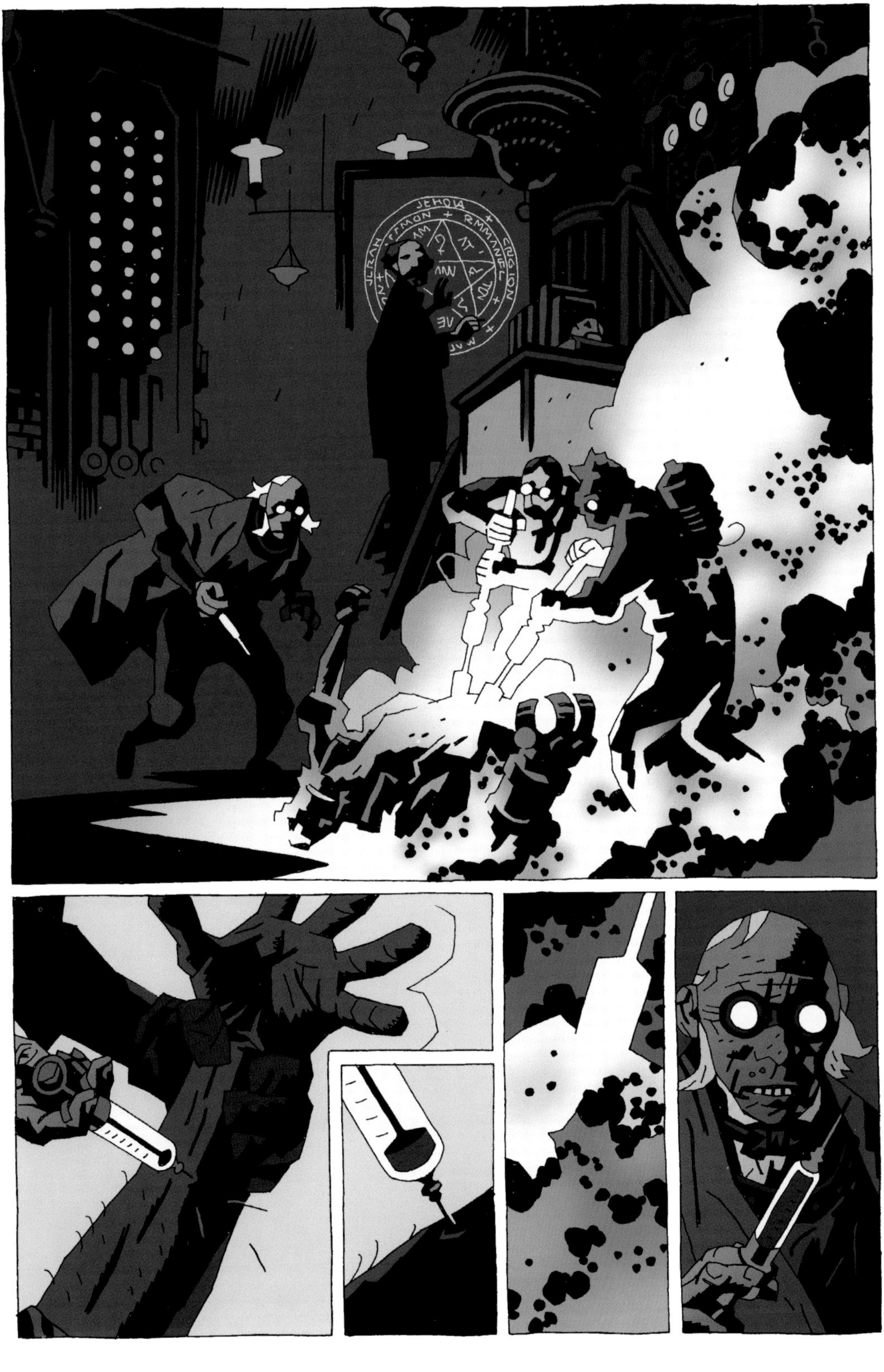

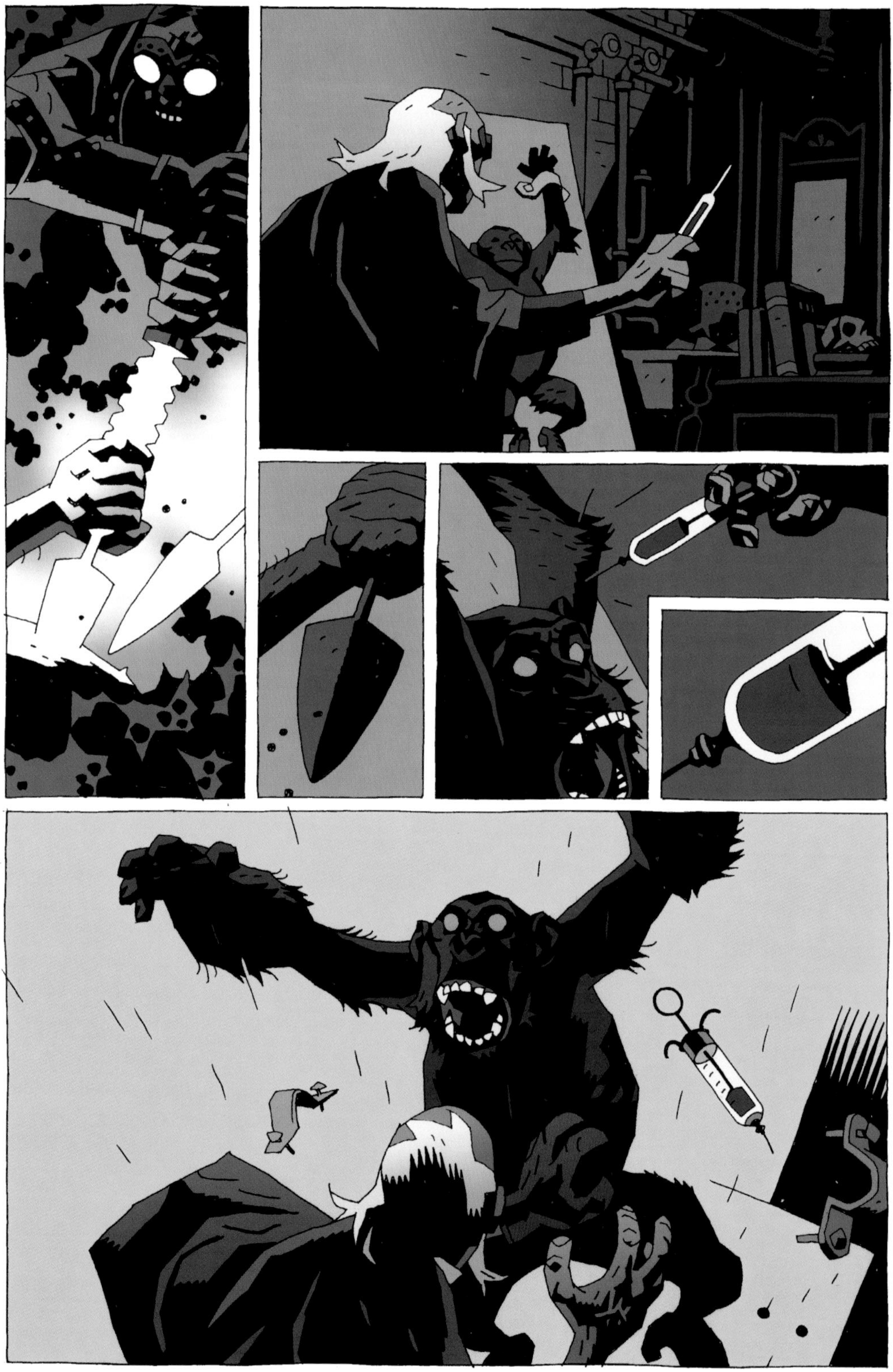

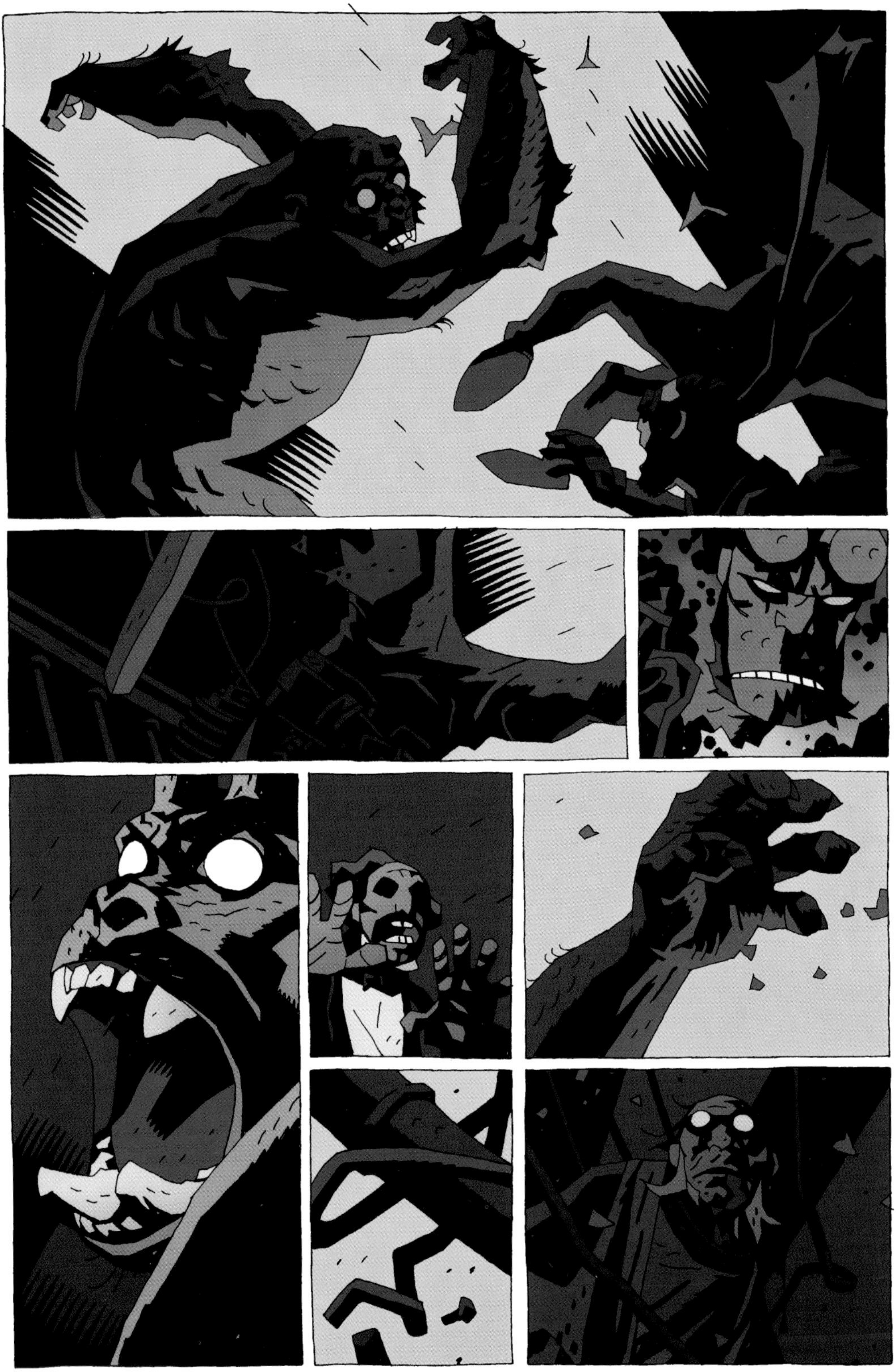

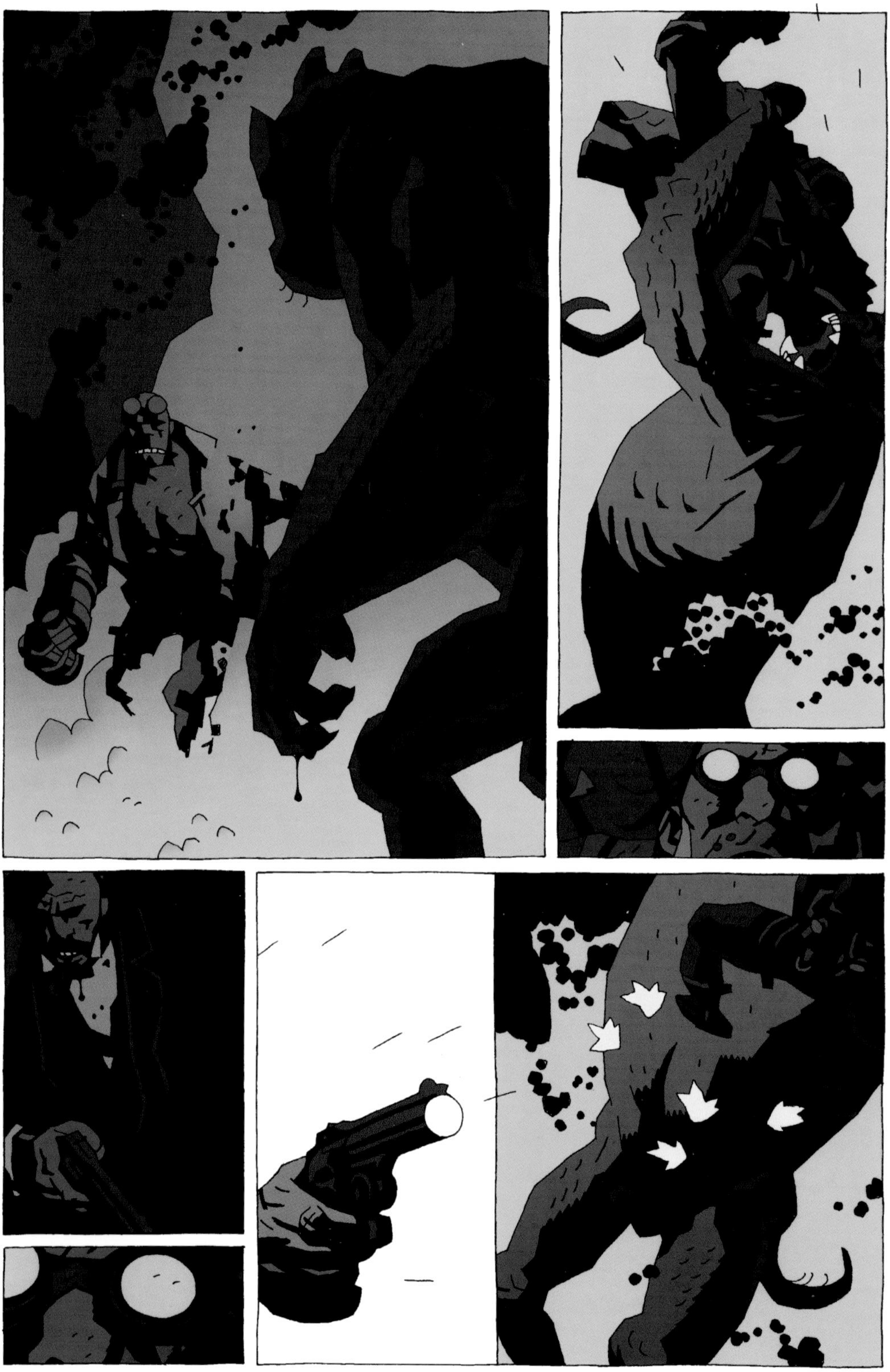

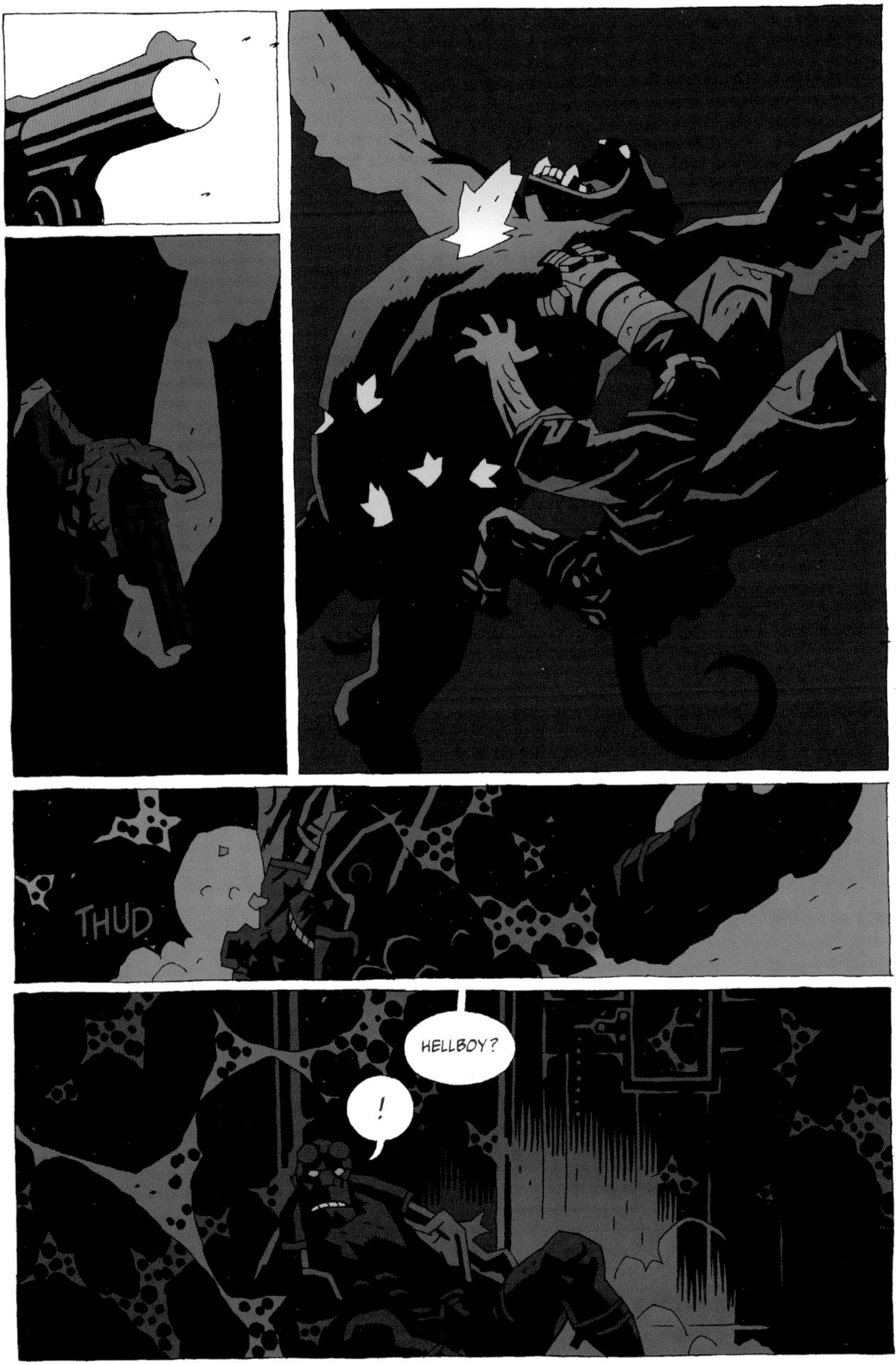

THUD
HELLBOY?
!

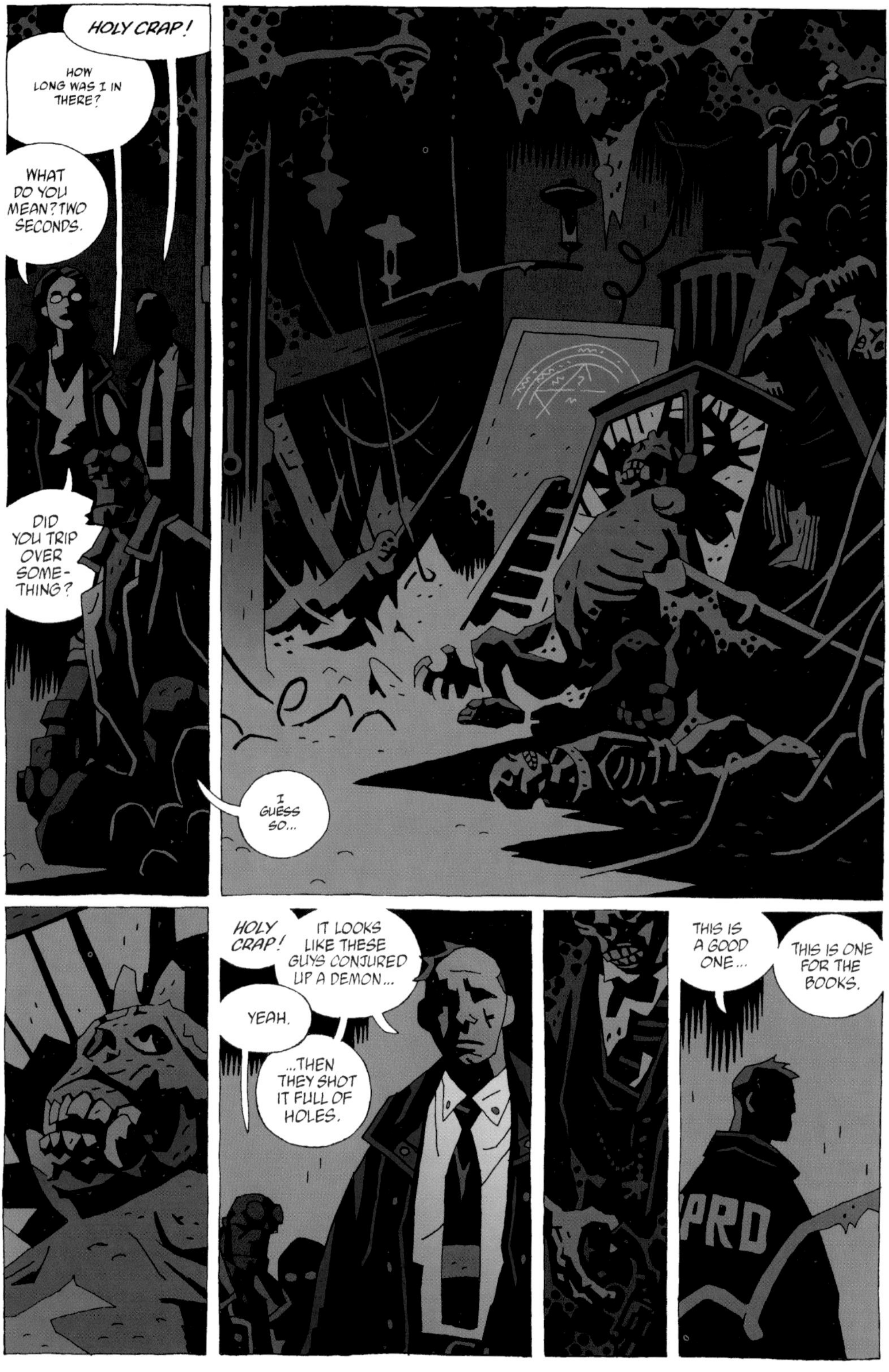
HOLY CRAP!
HOW LONG WAS I IN THERE?
WHAT DO YOU MEAN? TWO SECONDS.
DID YOU TRIP OVER SOME-THING?
I GUESS SO...
HOLY CRAP!
IT LOOKS LIKE THESE GUYS CONJURED UP A DEMON...
YEAH.
...THEN THEY SHOT IT FULL OF HOLES.
THIS IS A GOOD ONE...
THIS IS ONE FOR THE BOOKS.
PRD

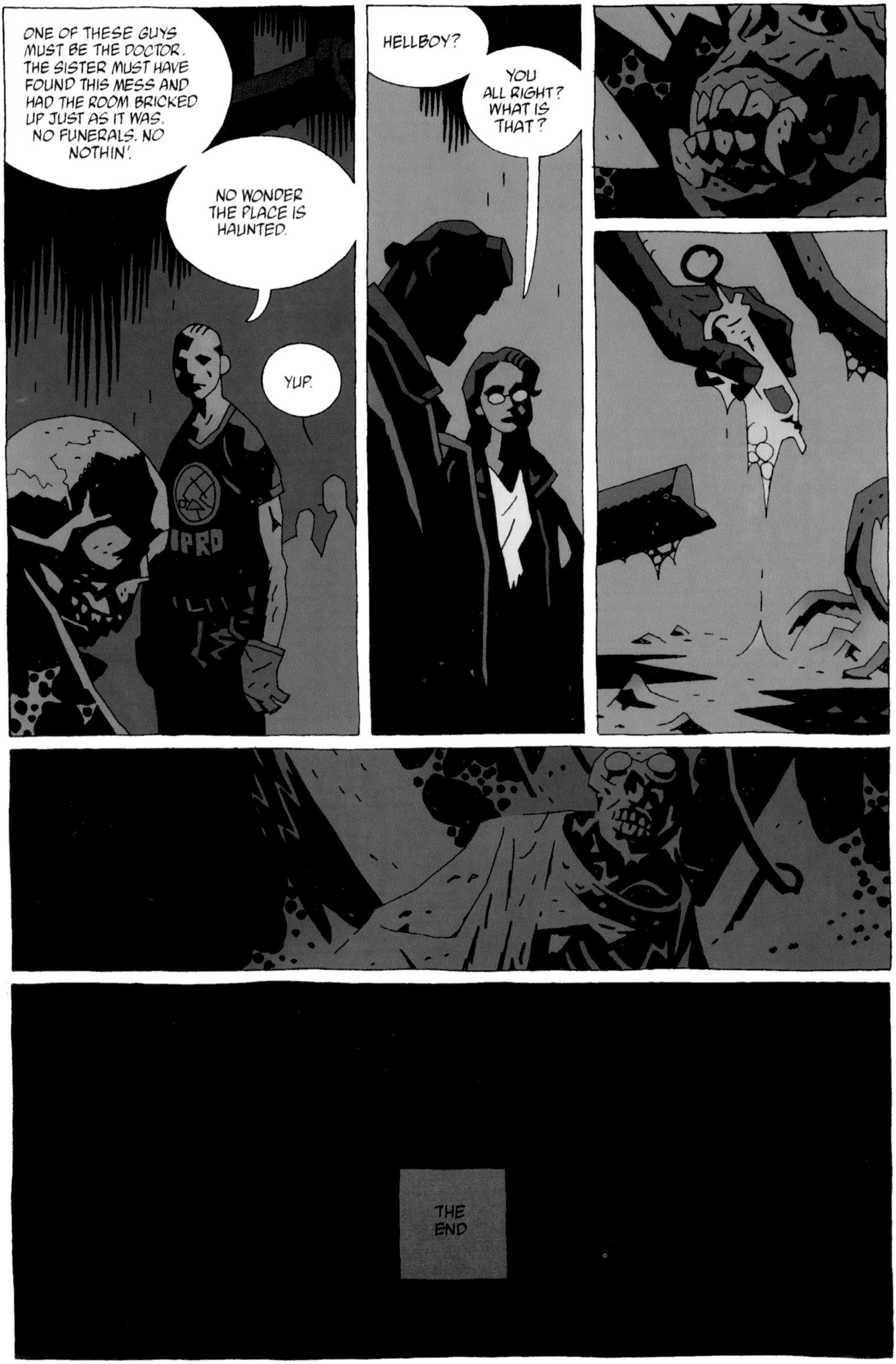
ONE OF THESE GUYS MUST BE THE DOCTOR. THE SISTER MUST HAVE FOUND THIS MESS AND HAD THE ROOM BRICKED UP JUST AS IT WAS. NO FUNERALS. NO NOTHIN'.
NO WONDER THE PLACE IS HAUNTED.
YUP.
HELLBOY?
YOU ALL RIGHT? WHAT IS THAT?
THE END

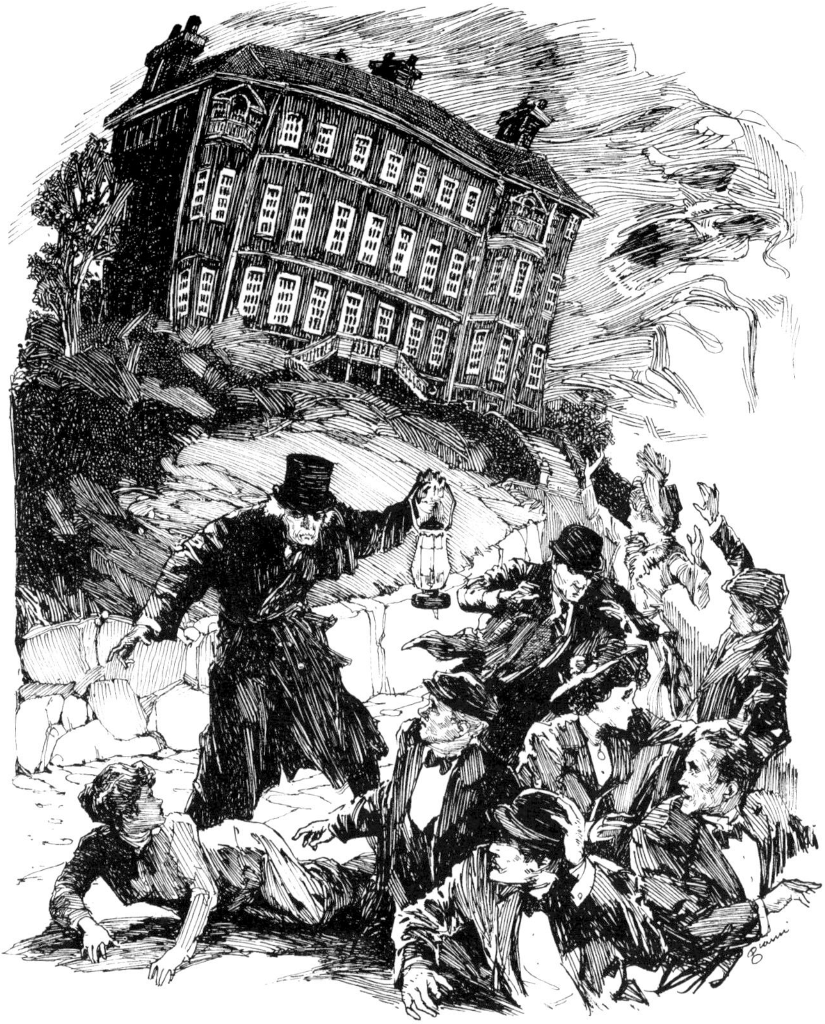

Thurnley Abbey

by PERCEVAL LANDON

ILLUSTRATIONS *by* GARY GIANNI

Three years ago I was on my way out to the East, and as an extra day in London was of some importance, I took the Friday evening mail-train to Brindisi instead of the usual Thursday morning Marseilles express. Many people shrink from the long, forty-eight-hour train journey through Europe, and the subsequent rush across the Mediterranean on the nineteen-knot *Isis* or *Osiris*; but there is really very little discomfort on either the train or the mail-boat, and unless there is actually nothing for me to do, I always like to save the extra day and a half in London. This time—it was early in the shipping season, probably about the beginning of September—there were few passengers, and I had a compartment to myself in the P. & O. Indian Express all the way from Calais. The journey was just like any other. We slept after luncheon; we dawdled the afternoon away with yellow-backed novels; sometimes we exchanged platitudes in the smoking room, and it was there that I met Alastair Colvin.

Colvin was a man of middle height, with a resolute, well-cut jaw; his hair was turning grey; his moustache was sun whitened, but otherwise he was clean-shaven—obviously a gentleman, and obviously also a preoccupied man. He had no great wit. When spoken to, he made the usual remarks in the right way, and I dare say he refrained from banalities only because he spoke less than the rest of us.

Of course this did not seem to me to be of any importance. Most travelers by train become a trifle infirm of purpose after thirty-six hours' rattling. But Colvin's restless way I noticed in somewhat marked contrast with the man's personal importance and dignity, especially ill suited to his finely made large hand with strong, broad, regular nails and its few lines. As I looked at his hand I noticed a long, deep, and recent scar of ragged shape. However, it is absurd to pretend that I thought anything was unusual. I went off at five o'clock on Sunday afternoon to sleep away the hour or two that had still to be got through before we arrived at Brindisi.

Once there, we few passengers transhipped our hand baggage, verified our berths—there were only a score of us in all—and then, after an aimless ramble of half an hour in Brindisi, we returned to dinner at the Hotel International, not wholly surprised that the town had been the death of Virgil. After dinner I was looking with awe at a trellis overgrown with blue vines, when Colvin moved across the room to my table. He picked up *Il Secolo*, but almost immediately gave up the pretence of reading it. He turned squarely to me and said:

"Would you do me a favour?"

One doesn't do favours to stray acquaintances on Continental expresses without knowing something more of them than I knew of Colvin. But I smiled in a noncommittal way, and asked him what he wanted. I wasn't wrong in part of my estimate of him; he said bluntly:

"Will you let me sleep in your cabin on the *Osiris*?" And he coloured a little as he said it.

Now, there is nothing more tiresome than having to put up with a stable companion at sea, and I asked him rather pointedly:

"Surely there is room for all of us?" I thought that perhaps he had been partnered off with some mangy Levantine, and wanted to escape from him at all hazards.

Colvin, still somewhat
confused, said, "Yes, I am in a cabin by myself. But you
would do me the greatest favour if you would allow me to share yours."

This was all very well, but, besides the fact that I always sleep better when
alone, there had been some recent thefts onboard English liners, and I
hesitated, frank and honest and self-conscious as Colvin was. Just then the
mail-train came in with a clatter and a rush of escaping steam, and I asked
him to see me again about it on the boat when we started. He answered me
curtly—I suppose he saw the mistrust in my manner—"I am a member of
White's." I smiled to myself as he said it, but I remembered in a moment that
the man—if he were really what he claimed to be, and I make no doubt that
he was—must have been sorely put to it before he urged that fact as a
guarantee of his respectability to a total stranger at a Brindisi hotel.

That evening, as we cleared the red and green harbor lights of Brindisi,
Colvin explained. This is his story in his own words.

"When I was traveling in India some years ago, I made the acquaintance
of a youngish man in the Woods and Forests. We camped out together for a
week, and I found him a pleasant companion. John Broughton was a light-
hearted soul when off duty, but a steady and capable man in any of the small
emergencies that continually arise in that department. He was liked and
trusted by the natives, and though a trifle over-pleased with himself when he
escaped to civilization at Simla or Calcutta, Broughton's future was well
assured in government service, when a fair-sized estate was unexpectedly

left to him, and he joyfully shook the dust of the Indian plains from his feet and returned to England. For five years he drifted about London. I saw him now and then. We dined together about every eighteen months, and I could trace pretty exactly the gradual sickening of Broughton with a merely idle life. At last he told me that he had decided to marry and settle down at his place, Thurnley Abbey, which had long been empty. He spoke about looking after the property and standing for his constituency in the usual way. Vivien Wilde, his fiancée, had, I suppose, begun to take him in hand.

"Among other things, I asked him about Thurnley Abbey. He confessed that he hardly knew the place. The last tenant, a man called Clarke, had lived in one wing for fifteen years and seen no one. He had been a miser and a hermit. It was the rarest thing for a light to be seen at the Abbey after dark. Only the barest necessities of life were ordered, and the tenant himself received them at the side door. His one half-caste manservant, after a month's stay in the house, had abruptly left without warning, and had returned to the Southern States. One thing Broughton complained bitterly about: Clarke had wilfully spread the rumor among the villagers that the Abbey was haunted, and had even condescended to play childish tricks with spirit-lamps and salt in order to scare trespassers away at night. He had been detected in the act of this tomfoolery, but the story spread, and no one, said Broughton, would venture near the house except in broad daylight. The hauntedness of Thurnley Abbey was now, he said with a grin, part of the gospel of the countryside, but he and his young wife were going to change all that. Would I propose myself any time I liked? I, of course, said I would, and equally, of course, intended to do nothing of the sort without a definite invitation.

"The house was put in thorough repair, though not a stick of the old furniture and tapestry was removed. Floors and ceilings were relaid; the roof was made watertight again, and the dust of half a century was scoured out. It was called an Abbey, though as a matter of fact it had been only the infirmary of the long-vanished Abbey of Clouster some five miles away. The larger part of the building remained as it had been in pre-Reformation days, but a wing had been added in Jacobean times, and that part of the house had been kept in something like repair by Mr. Clarke. He had, in both the ground and first floors, set heavy timber doors, strongly barred with iron, in the passage between the earlier and the Jacobean parts of the house, and had entirely neglected the former. So there had been a good deal of work to be done.

"Broughton, whom I saw in London two or three times about this period, made a deal of fun over the positive refusal of the workmen to remain after sundown. Even after electric light had been put into every room, nothing would induce them to remain, though, as Broughton observed, electric light was death on ghosts. The legend of the Abbey's ghosts had gone far and wide,

and the men would take no risks. They went home in batches of five and six, and even during the daylight hours there was an inordinate amount of talking between one another, if either happened to be out of sight of his companion. On the whole, though nothing of any sort had been conjured up even by their heated imaginations during their five months' work upon the Abbey, the belief in the ghosts was rather strengthened than otherwise because of the men's confessed nervousness, and local tradition declared itself in favor of the ghost of an immured nun.

"'Good old nun!' said Broughton.

"I asked him whether in general he believed in the possibility of ghosts, and, rather to my surprise, he said that he couldn't say he entirely disbelieved in them. A man in India had told him one morning in camp that he believed that his mother was dead in England, as her vision had come to his tent the night before. He had not been alarmed, but had said nothing, and the figure vanished again. As a matter of fact, the next possible *dak-walla* brought on a telegram announcing the mother's death. 'There the thing was,' said Broughton. But at Thurnley he was practical enough. He roundly cursed the idiotic selfishness of Clarke, whose silly antics had caused all the inconvenience. At the same time, he couldn't refuse to sympathize to some extent with the ignorant workmen. 'My own idea,' said he, 'is that if a ghost ever does come in one's way, one ought to speak to it.'

"I agreed. Little as I knew of the ghost world and its conventions, I had always remembered that a spook was honor bound to wait to be spoken to. It didn't seem much to do, and I felt that the sound of one's own voice would at any rate reassure oneself as to one's wakefulness. But there are few ghosts outside Europe—few, that is, that a white man can see—and I had never been troubled with any. However, as I have said, I told Broughton that I agreed.

"So the wedding took place, and I went to it in a tall hat which I bought for the occasion, and the new Mrs. Broughton smiled very nicely at me afterwards. As it had to happen, I took the Orient Express that evening and was not in England again for nearly six months. Just before I came back, I got a letter from Broughton. He asked if I could see him in London or come to Thurnley, as he thought I should be better able to help him than anyone else he knew. I had nothing to do, so after dealing with some small accumulation of business during my absence, I packed a kit-bag and departed to Euston. I was met by Broughton's great limousine at Thurnley Road station, and after a drive of nearly seven miles, I could see the Abbey across a wide pasturage.

"Broughton had seen me coming from afar, and walked across from his other guests to welcome me. There was no doubt that the man was altered, gravely altered. He was nervous and fidgety, and I found him looking at me only when my eye was off him. I naturally asked him what he wanted of me. I told him I would do anything I could, but that I couldn't conceive what he lacked that I could provide. He said with a lusterless smile that there was, however, something, and that he would tell me the following morning. It struck me that he was somehow ashamed of himself, and perhaps ashamed of the part he was asking me to play. However, I dismissed the subject from my mind and went up to dress in my palatial room.

"It was a very large low room with oak beams projecting from the white ceiling. Every inch of the walls, including the doors, was covered with tapestry, and a remarkably fine Italian fourpost bedstead, heavily draped, added to the darkness and dignity of the place. All the furniture was old, well made, and dark. Underfoot there was a plain green pile carpet, the only new thing about the room except the electric-light fittings and the jugs and basins. Even the looking glass on the dressing table was an old pyramidal Venetian glass set in a heavy repoussé frame of tarnished silver.

"After a few minutes' cleaning up, I went downstairs. Nothing much happened at dinner. The people were very much like those of the garden party. A young

woman next to me
seemed anxious to know what
was being read in London. As she was
far more familiar than I with the most recent magazines and literary
supplements, I found salvation in being myself instructed in the tendencies of
modern fiction. She was a cheerless soul, yet nothing could have been less
creepy than the glitter of silver and glass, and the subdued lights and cackle of
conversation all around the dinner table.

"After the ladies had gone I found myself talking to the rural dean. He
was a thin, earnest man, who at once turned the conversation to old
Clarke's buffooneries. But, he said, Mr. Broughton had introduced such a
new and cheerful spirit, not only into the Abbey, but, he might say, into the
whole neighbourhood, that he had great hopes that the ignorant
superstitions of the past were henceforth destined to oblivion. Thereupon
his other neighbour, a portly gentleman of independent means and
position, audibly remarked, 'Amen,' which damped the rural dean, and we
talked of partridges past, partridges present, and pheasants to come. At the
other end of the table Broughton sat with a couple of his friends, red-faced
hunting men. Once I noticed that they were discussing me, but I paid no
attention to it at the time. I remembered it a few hours later.

"By eleven all the guests were gone, and Broughton, his wife, and I were
alone together under the fine plaster ceiling of the Jacobean drawing room.
Mrs. Broughton talked about one or two of the neighbours, and then, with

a smile, said that she knew I would excuse her, shook hands with me, and went off to bed. I am not very good at analyzing things, but I felt that she talked a little uncomfortably and with a suspicion of effort, smiled rather conventionally, and was obviously glad to go. These things seem trifling enough to repeat, but I had the faint feeling that everything was not quite square. Under the circumstances, this was enough to set me wondering what on earth the service could be that I was to render—wondering also whether the whole business were not some ill-advised jest in order to make me come down from London for a mere shooting party.

"Broughton said little after she had gone. But he was evidently laboring to bring the conversation around to the so-called haunting of the Abbey. As soon as I saw this, of course I asked him directly about it. He then seemed at once to lose interest in the matter. There was no doubt about it: Broughton was somehow a changed man, and to my mind he had changed in no way for the better. Mrs. Broughton seemed no sufficient cause. He was clearly very fond of her, and she of him. I reminded him that he was going to tell me what I could do for him in the morning, pleaded my journey, lit a candle, and went upstairs with him. At the end of the passage leading into the old house he grinned weakly and said, 'Mind, if you see a ghost, do talk to it; you said you would.' He stood irresolutely a moment and then turned away. At the door of his dressing room he paused once more: 'I'm here,' he called out, 'if you should want anything. Good night,' and he shut the door.

"I went along the passage to my room, undressed, switched on a lamp beside my bed, read a few pages of *The Jungle Book*, and then, more than ready for sleep, turned the light off and went fast asleep.

"Three hours later I woke up. There was not a breath of wind outside. There was not even a flicker of light from the fireplace. As I lay there, an ash tinkled slightly as it cooled, but there was hardly a gleam of the dullest red in the grate. An owl cried among the silent Spanish chestnuts on the slope outside. I idly reviewed the events of the day, hoping that I should fall off to sleep again before I reached dinner. But at the end I seemed as wakeful as ever. There was no help for it. I must read my *Jungle Book* again till I felt ready to go off, so I fumbled for the pear at the end of the cord that hung down inside the bed, and I switched on the bedside lamp. The sudden glory dazzled me for a moment. I felt under my pillow for my book with half-shut eyes. Then, growing used to the light, I happened to look down to the foot of my bed.

"I can never tell you really what happened then. Nothing I could ever confess in the most abject words could even faintly picture to you what I felt. I know that my heart stopped dead, and my throat shut automatically. In one instinctive movement I crouched back up against the headboards of the bed, staring at the horror. The movement set my heart going again, and the sweat dripped from every pore. I am not a particularly religious man, but I

had always believed that God would never allow any supernatural appearance to present itself to man in such a guise and in such circumstances that harm, either bodily or mental, could result to him. I can only tell you that at the moment both my life and my reason rocked unsteadily on their seats."

The other *Osiris* passengers had gone to bed. Only Colvin and I remained leaning over the starboard railing, which rattled uneasily now and then under the fierce vibration of the over-engined mail boat. Far over, there were the lights of a few fishing smacks riding out the night, and a great rush of white combing and seething water fell out and away from us overside.

At last Colvin went on:

"Leaning over the foot of my bed, looking at me, was a figure swathed in a rotten and tattered veiling. This shroud passed over the head, but left both eyes and the right side of the face bare. It then followed the line of the arm down to where the hand grasped the bed end. The face was not entirely that of a skull, though the eyes and the flesh of the face were totally gone. There was a thin, dry skin drawn tightly over the features, and there was some skin left on the hand. One wisp of hair crossed the forehead. It was perfectly still. I looked at it, and it looked at me, and my brains turned dry and hot in my head. I had still got the pear of the electric lamp in my hand, and I played idly with it; only I dared not turn the light out again. I shut my eyes, only to open them in a hideous terror the same second. The thing had not moved.

My heart was thumping, and the sweat cooled me as it evaporated. Another cinder tinkled in the grate, and a panel creaked in the wall.

"My reason failed me. For twenty minutes, or twenty seconds, I was able to think of nothing else but this awful figure, till there came, hurtling through the empty channels of my senses, the remembrances that Broughton and his friends had discussed with me furtively at dinner. The dim possibility of it being a hoax stole gratefully into my unhappy mind, and once there, pluck came creeping back along a thousand tiny veins. My first sensation was one of blind unreasoning thankfulness that my brain was going to stand the trial. I am not a timid man, but the best of us needs some human handle to steady him in time of extremity, and in this faint but growing hope that it might be only a brutal hoax, I found the fulcrum that I needed. At last I moved.

"How I managed to do it I cannot tell you, but with one spring toward the foot of the bed I got within arm's length and struck out one fearful blow with my fist at the thing. It crumbled under it, and my hand was cut to the bone. With a sickening revulsion after my terror, I dropped half-fainting across the end of the bed. So it was merely a foul trick after all. No doubt the trick had been played many a time before: no doubt Broughton and his friends had had some large bet among themselves as to what I should do when I discovered the gruesome thing. From my state of abject terror I found myself transported into an insensate anger. I shouted curses upon Broughton. I

dived rather than climbed over the bed-end of the sofa. I tore at the robed skeleton—how well the whole thing had been carried out, I thought—I broke the skull against the floor, and stamped upon its dry bones. I flung the head away under the bed, and rent the brittle bones of the trunk in pieces. I snapped the thin thigh bones across my knee, and flung them in different directions. The shin bones I set up against a stool and broke with my heel. I raged like a berserker against the loathly thing, and stripped the ribs from the backbone and slung the breastbone against the cupboard. My fury increased as the work of destruction went on. I tore the frail rotten veil into twenty pieces, and the dust went up over everything, over the clean blotting paper and the silver inkstand. At last my work was done. There was but a raffle of broken bones and strips of parchment and crumbling wool. Then, picking up a piece of the skull—it was the cheek and temple bone of the right side, I remember—I opened the door and went down the passage to Broughton's dressing room. I remember still how my sweat-dripping pajamas clung to me as I walked. At the door I kicked and entered.

"Broughton was in bed. He had already turned the light on and seemed shrunken and horrified. For a moment he could hardly pull himself together. Then I spoke. I don't know what I said. I know only that from a heart full and over full with hatred and contempt, spurred on by shame of my own recent cowardice, I let my tongue run on. He answered nothing. I was amazed at my own fluency. My hair still clung lankly to my wet temples, my hand was bleeding profusely, and I must have looked a strange sight. Broughton huddled himself at the head of the bed just as I had. Still he made no answer, no defense. He seemed preoccupied with something besides my reproaches, and once or twice moistened his lips with his tongue. He could say nothing, though he moved his hands now and then, just as a baby who cannot speak moves its hands.

"At last the door into Mrs. Broughton's rooms opened and she came in, white and terrified. 'What is it? What is it? Oh, in God's name! What is it?' she cried again and again, and then she went up to her husband and sat on the bed in her night-dress, and the two faced me. I told her what the matter was. I spared her husband not a word for her presence there. Yet he seemed hardly to understand. I told the pair that I had spoiled their cowardly joke for them. Broughton looked up.

"'I have smashed the foul thing into a hundred pieces,' I said. Broughton licked his lips again and his mouth worked. 'By God!' I shouted, 'it would serve you right if I thrashed you within an inch of your life. I will take care that not a decent man or woman of my acquaintance ever speaks to you again. And there,' I added, throwing the broken piece of the skull upon the floor beside his bed, 'there is a souvenir for you, of your damned work tonight!'

"Broughton saw the bone, and in a moment it was his turn to frighten me. He squealed like a hare caught in a trap. He screamed and screamed till Mrs. Broughton, almost as bewildered as myself, held on to him and coaxed him like a child to be quiet. But Broughton—and as he moved I thought that ten minutes ago I perhaps looked as terribly ill as he did—thrust her from him, and scrambled out of bed on to the floor, and, still screaming, put out his hand to the bone. It had blood on it from my hand. He paid no attention to me whatever. In truth I said nothing. This was a new turn indeed to the horrors of the evening. He rose from the floor with the bone in his hand and stood silent. He seemed to be listening. 'Time, time, perhaps,' he muttered, and almost at the same moment fell at full length on the carpet, cutting his head against the fender. The bone flew from his hand and came to rest near the door. I picked Broughton up, haggard and broken, with blood over his face. He whispered hoarsely and quickly, 'Listen, listen!' We listened.

"After ten seconds' utter quiet, I seemed to hear something. I could not be sure, but at last there was no doubt. There was a quiet sound as one moving along the passage. Little regular steps came toward us over the hard oak flooring. Broughton moved to where his wife sat, white and speechless, on the bed, and pressed her face into his shoulder.

"Then—the last thing that I could see as he turned the light out—he fell forward with his own head pressed into the pillow of the bed. Something in their company, something in their cowardice, helped me, and I faced the open doorway of the room, which was outlined fairly clearly against the dimly lit passage. I put out one hand and touched Mrs. Broughton's shoulder in the darkness, but at the last moment I too failed. I sank on my knees and put my face in the bed. Only we all heard. The footsteps came to the door and there they stopped. The piece of bone was lying a yard inside the door. There was a rustle of moving stuff, and the thing was in the room. Mrs. Broughton was silent: I could hear Broughton's voice praying, muffled in the pillow. I was cursing my own cowardice. Then the steps moved out again on the oak boards of the passage, and I heard the sounds dying away. In a flash of remorse I went to the door and looked out. At the end of the corridor I thought I saw something that moved away. A moment later the passage was empty. I stood with my forehead against the jamb of the door almost physically sick.

"'You can turn the light on,' I said, and there was an answering flare. There was no bone at my feet. Mrs. Broughton had fainted. Broughton was almost useless, and it took me ten minutes to bring her to. Broughton only said one thing worth remembering. For the most part he went on muttering prayers. But I was glad afterwards to recollect that he had said that thing. He said in a colourless voice, half as a question, half as a reproach, 'You didn't speak to her.'

"We spent the remainder of the night together. Mrs. Broughton actually fell off into a kind of sleep before dawn, but she suffered so horribly in her dreams that I shook her into consciousness again. Never was dawn so long in coming. Three or four times Broughton spoke to himself. Mrs. Broughton would then just tighten her hold on his arm, but she could say nothing. As for me, I can honestly say that I grew worse as the hours passed and the light strengthened. The two violent reactions had battered down my steadiness of view, and I felt that the foundations of my life had been built upon the sand. I said nothing, and after binding up my hand with a towel, I did not move. It was better so. They helped me and I helped them, and we all three knew that our reason had gone very near to ruin that night. At last, when the light came in pretty strongly, and the birds outside were chattering and singing, we felt that we must do something. Yet we never moved. You might have thought that we should particularly dislike being found as we were by the servants, yet nothing of that kind mattered a straw, and an overpowering listlessness bound us as we sat, until Chapman, Broughton's man, actually knocked and opened the door. None of us moved. Broughton,

speaking hardly and stiffly, said, 'Chapman, you can come back in five minutes.' Chapman was a discreet man, but it would have made no difference to us if he had carried his news to the 'room' at once.

"We looked at each other and I said I must go back. I meant to wait outside till Chapman returned. I simply dared not re-enter my bedroom alone. Broughton roused himself and said that he would come with me. Mrs. Broughton agreed to remain in her own room for five minutes if the blinds were drawn up and all the doors left open.

"So Broughton and I, leaning stiffly one against the other, went down to my room. By the morning light that filtered past the blinds we could see our way, and I released the blinds. There was nothing wrong with the room from end to end, except smears of my own blood on the end of the bed, on the sofa, and on the carpet where I had torn the thing to pieces."

Colvin had finished his story. There was nothing to say. Seven bells stuttered out from the fo'c's'le, and the answering cry wailed through the darkness. I took him downstairs.

"Of course I am much better now, but it is a kindness of you to let me sleep in your cabin."

The End

WAH AHUH AH AHH
DING DONG
AH AUHAH WAH
AHUH AH AH WAH UH
IT'S ABOUT &@-;-;-#ING TIME!
THIS SMALL FAVOR
ALLIE, LEE, HORTON & STEWART
WAHH AHUH AUHUH AHUH

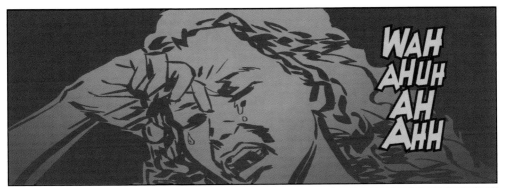

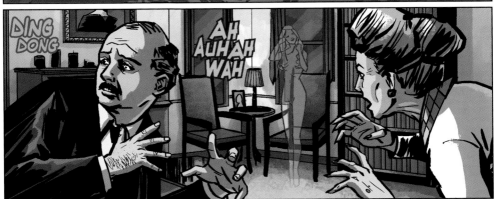

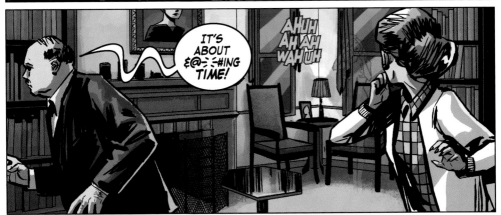

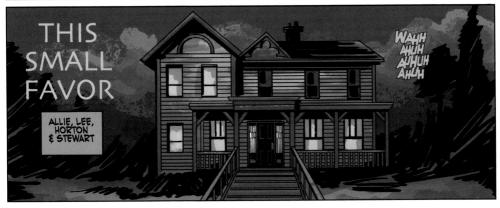

PEST CONTROL.
YOU'RE LATE! IF-IF YOU'D GOTTEN HERE WHEN YOU'D SAID YOU--!
EXCUSE ME?!? I DON'T HAVE TO HELP YOU--
NO, NO--PLEASE, MR. WAITE--THIS WAY. MY WIFE'S IN THE PARLOR ... SHE ... WELL, YOU, ah, YOU KNOW HOW WOMEN ARE ... LET ME GIVE YOU THE BASIC FACTS, AND YOU CAN BEGIN.
IT'S A GOOD HOUSE--WELL, YOU CAN SEE THAT.
IT WAS BUILT FOR THE HOBBS SISTERS--TWO WEALTHY SPINSTERS. ONE WENT MISSING, THE OTHER RAN OFF TO BE MARRIED. EVER SINCE, RESIDENTS HAVE BEEN PLAGUED BY GHOSTLY SOBS ... WEIRD DRIPPINGS.
IN 1959, THE NEW OWNER, THE POET SPENCER SALMON-CROUSE DIED IN THE KITCHEN AFTER DISCOVERING THE BODY OF THE MISSING HOBBS WOMAN --SHE'D BEEN KILLED, ONE CAN ASSUME, BY HER SISTER.
THEN THERE WAS THE WIDOWER ...

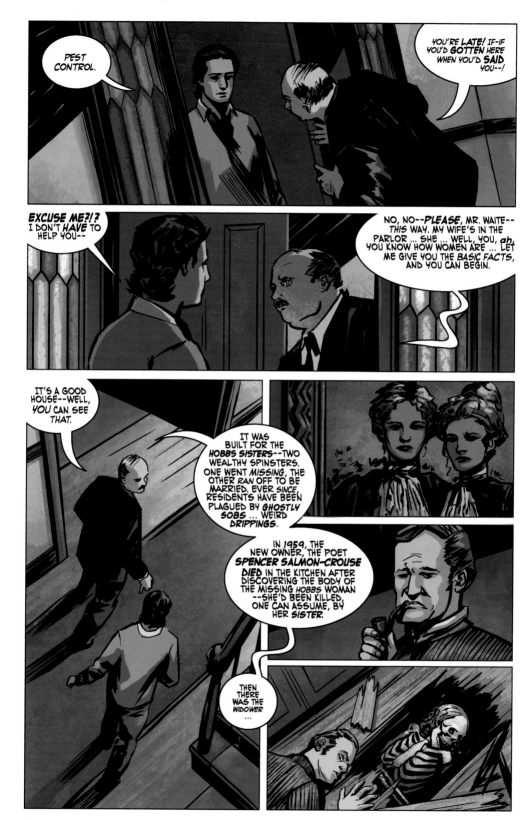

"HE WOKE ONE NIGHT TO SEE *THE SPIRIT* STANDING BEFORE HIS LATE WIFE'S DRESSER. SHE SLIPPED RIGHT INTO HIS BED, GIVING THE OLD DOG A *HEART ATTACK*. Heh heh ..."

"WAIT A SECOND, MR. MATTHIES--HOW DO YOU KNOW WHAT HE SAW IF HE DIED?"

"HE *DIDN'T*. HE TOLD EVERYONE THAT ONCE HE WAS WELL, HE WOULD 'TAKE THE YOUNG LADY UP ON HER OFFER!' A SPINSTER IN *HER* DAY, BUT SHE LOOKED ALL RIGHT TO HIM!"

"HE, *ah*, HE HAD ANOTHER HEART ATTACK THAT FIRST NIGHT HOME."

YOU SAID ON THE PHONE THAT YOU HAVE KIDS.

WE SENT THE POOR THINGS TO STAY WITH *FRIENDS* TONIGHT ...

WE'RE PROPER CHRISTIANS, MR. WAITE.

MY WIFE. FRANCES.

I DIDN'T WANT MY GIRLS EXPOSED TO *WHATEVER IT IS* YOU'RE ABOUT TO DO.

WELL, MR. AND MRS. MATTHIES--SOUNDS LIKE THIS *GHOST'S* REALLY CONNECTED TO THE HOUSE. I MEAN, IT *MUST BE MISS HOBBS*, RIGHT? DON'T YOU THINK SHE KIND OF ADDS TO THE *HISTORY* OF THE PLACE...?

CERTAINLY DOESN'T ADD TO THE PROPERTY VALUES.

ONE *MIGHT* SAY THAT *CARPENTER ANTS* ARE GOD'S CREATURES, BUT THAT DOESN'T MEAN I WANT THEM IN MY *KITCHEN*.

I ASSURE YOU THIS SPIRIT'S ANTICS ARE *QUITE* INTOLERABLE, MR. WAITE.

YOU MEAN LIKE THIS?

?!
FWOOOSH
AIIIE!
AHHHHHH
IT'S HORRIBLE!
YOD HEH VAU HEH!

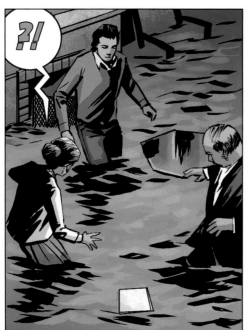

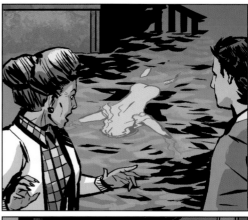

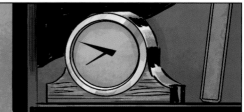

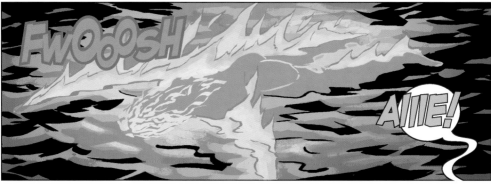

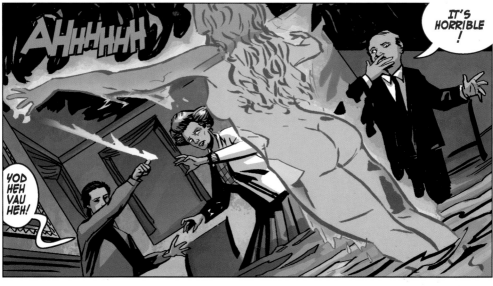

ADONAI ...
NOOOOO
...
AHUH
WAH HUH
WHAT THE &@*!# ARE YOU WAITING FOR?!?
HUHH AHUH AHUH
YEE!
SMASH
RELAX! THIS IS NORMAL! IT'LL GET A LOT WORSE!
ERHEBET EUCH, OH IHR GEISTER, DAS FRAULEIN HOBBS UND AUCH DER DICHTER SALMON-CROUSE!
ICH RUFE EUCH AN IN DEN HOCHHEILIGEN NAMEN, YIAI, EHEIEH UND AUCH ANACHIEL.

EEEEE!!
THAT'S RIGHT, DEAR FRANCES-- THE WOMAN'S PLACE IS IN THE KITCHEN.
This isn't happening this isn't happening ...
LASSET STURM WUTEN!
TREIBET EURE FEINDE VOR EUCH AUS DIESEM LAND!
Whoooosh
SPLASH

CRASH
CRACK
gasp
HEH HEH HEH ...

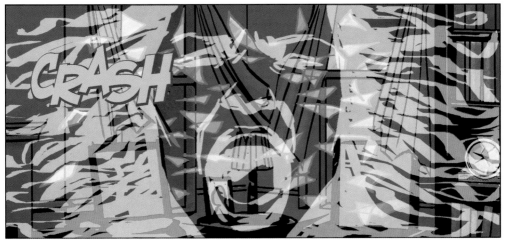

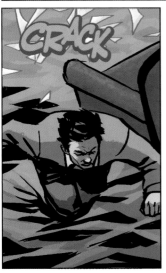

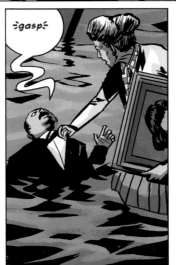

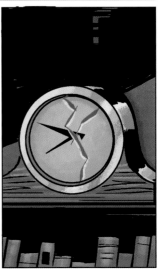

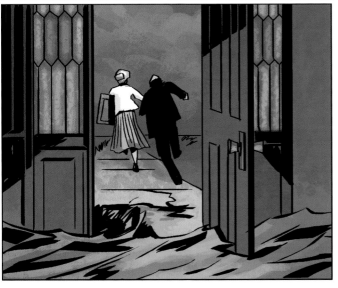

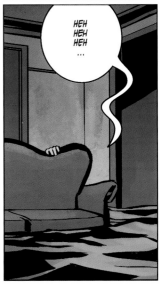

WELL, YOU DON'T HAVE TO WORRY ABOUT *THOSE* TWO COMING BACK.
THANK YOU
HOLD *ON* A SEC-- WHAT WAS THE IDEA GETTING IN THAT OLD MAN'S BED?
FAIR ENOUGH.
SORRY I DRAGGED YOU INTO THIS, *MR. SALMON-CROUSE*. I FIGURED *MISS HOBBS* JUST NEEDED A LITTLE HELP DRIVING THOSE TWO OUT.
Ah! WOULDN'T'VE MISSED IT.
THE END

SPECIAL THANKS TO GUNTHER NICKEL

FOREVER
©2003 ULI OESTERLE
BZZZZZ
DOCTOR LE
OPEN
ORIGINAL CHINESE
TATT
HAMBU
ST. PAULI
HEY!
ORIGINA
CHINESE
TA
ORIGINAL
CHINESE
TATOOS
1

STOP! WAIT!
QUICK, GET GOING!
BUDDHA BUDDHA BUDDHA
VROOOOOM
?
HH-ME 245
SBOK
THUD
ASTRA

HE HE HE HE HE HE HE HE HE
HE FELL... WE OUGHTTA GO BACK.
DON'T BE RETARDED.
... WE BARELY TOUCHED HIM. HE'LL BE FINE.
AND WHAT IF HE SUES US?
SCREW HIM!
YOU BETTER CHECK THIS OUT --A REAL BARGAIN! SMART, EH?
UFT
GOD, YOU'RE A BASTARD!
KOF KOF
REVENGE!

OOPH
OOPH
OOPH
OOPH
ONE WEEK AND SEVERAL DISCUSSIONS LATER...
...MY SQUAW WAS BEGINNING TO GET ON MY NERVES.
YOU DIDN'T SEEM TO BE INTO IT, BABE. WHERE WERE YOU?
I KEEP THINKING OF THAT TATTOOIST. I HOPE HE'S OKAY.
OH, JESUS! DON'T BE SUCH A GIRL.
BUT I AM A GIRL.
AND, BY THE WAY... WASN'T YOUR TATTOO SMALLER?
I JUST COULDN'T STOP LAUGHING.
NEXT MORNING, I WASN'T LAUGHING ANYMORE.
MARLA WAS RIGHT.
IT WAS GETTING BIGGER, CRAWLING ACROSS MY SKIN LIKE A GREEDY, BLACK COCKROACH.
I WENT TO SEE A SPECIALIST, BUT HE COULDN'T MAKE ANY MORE SENSE OF IT THAN I COULD.
THEOBALD SKINNER DERMATOLOGIST

ANOTHER TWO WEEKS PASSED, AND IT JUST GOT WORSE. THE TATTOO COMPLETELY COVERED MY ARMS AND LEGS. I WAS FORCED TO WEAR A TURTLENECK-- AT THE HEIGHT OF SUMMER.

HOW'S THAT JOHNSON PROGRAM GOING?

SMASHING! FABULOUS! ABSOLUTELY FIRST-CLASS.

WELL, THAT SOUNDS PROMISING... ER, WHAT'S THIS ON YOUR HAND?

I WOULDN'T BE ABLE TO CONCEAL IT MUCH LONGER.

OH, IT'S NOTHING.

ZUP

MY GODDAMN SKIN CONDITION HAVING A LIFE OF ITS OWN RATHER SPOILED OUR SOCIAL LIFE.

I MOST SINCERELY APOLOGIZE, SIR, BUT WE MUST URGE YOU TO LEAVE THE PREMISES OF OUR RESTAURANT.

LISTEN, YOU PANSY FAGGOT, WE'RE REGULARS HERE.

NOT ANY MORE.

I PHONED IN SICK AND STOPPED GOING TO WORK.

AS A MATTER OF FACT, I DIDN'T GO ANYWHERE.

Dear Anton,
I cannot cope with this situation any longer.
I'm leaving you.
I once loved you but that's so long ago.
You are a Shithead.
Farewell, Karla.
I'VE BEEN A SELFISH JERK ALL MY LIFE, AND I'VE FINALLY RECEIVED THE BILL.
MY FRIENDS--THE FEW I HAD, ANYWAY--TOOK THIS OPPORTUNITY AND ENDED THEIR CONTACT WITH ME.
EVEN MY PARENTS WON'T HAVE ANYTHING TO DO WITH ME.
KLEP KLAP
LETTERS
I RECEIVED WRITTEN NOTIFICATION THAT I HAD LOST MY JOB, AND ANOTHER LETTER THREATENING ME WITH EVICTION FROM MY FLAT.
I WATCHED IN HORROR AS THE LAST CLEAR PATCHES OF MY SKIN FELL VICTIM TO THIS PLAGUE. MY LIFE AS I'VE KNOWN IT HAS TERMINATED.
I KNOW WHAT I HAVE TO DO.

IF DR. LEE WAS CAPABLE OF STARTING THIS THING IN MY BODY, HE SHOULD ALSO BE ABLE TO REVERSE IT. AND IF HE'S NOT WILLING, I HAVE SOME LEADEN ARGUMENTS ON MY SIDE.

ER, HI THERE... I'M LOOKING FOR CHENG LEE, THE TATTOO ARTIST.

HE DIED IN AN ACCIDENT A FEW WEEKS AGO.

...HE WAS MY FATHER...

...A CUSTOMER WHO DIDN'T WANT TO PAY HIT HIM WITH HIS CAR.

JESUS... I... I'M SORRY...

?

GOTTA GO!

HEF HEF HEF
BUTCH
DON'T.
I DIDN'T RECOGNIZE YOU AT FIRST... MAN, THAT'S DEFINITELY MY FATHER'S WORK.
IT WAS YOU, RIGHT? YOU KILLED MY OLD MAN?
YES, BUT...
IT WAS AN ACCIDENT. YOU ARE NOT TO BLAME.
MY FATHER WAS PISSED. UNDERSTANDABLY SO, RIGHT? THIS IS AN ANCIENT CURSE DATING BACK TO OUR FOREFATHERS.
I'M SORRY?
I CAN TAKE IT FROM YOU. MY FATHER TAUGHT ME EVERYTHING. EVERYTHING I NEED TO KNOW.
COME WITH ME...
"...THESE THINGS TAKE TIME."
LUCKILY, I PREVENTED THAT IDIOT FROM PUNCHING AN UGLY HOLE IN MY OLD MAN'S LAST WORK-- HIS BEST ONE, TOO. NOW THE MASTERPIECE IS SAFE, PRESERVED AS IT SHOULD BE, IN THE BOSOM OF THE VENERABLE LEE FAMILY.
8
OESTERLE 3/03

PFFT... I DON'T BELIEVE IN *GHOSTS*...
BUT GHOSTS ARE *EVERYWHERE.* YOU JUST NEED TO KNOW WHERE TO LOOK.
GGH!
COME THIS WAY AND LET ME SHOW YOU...
...The House On The Corner!
THIS HOME WAS BUILT IN 1882 AS A WEDDING PRESENT TO THE WOMAN WHO WOULD LIVE HERE. IT WAS CHERISHED DEARLY BY ITS RESIDENTS AND WAS EVENTUALLY PASSED DOWN FROM THE WOMAN TO HER DAUGHTERS.
THE HOUSE WAS OCCUPIED FOR EIGHTY-TWO YEARS, UNTIL THE LAST DAUGHTER DIED IN 1971. AFTER THAT IT SAT EMPTY FOR ANOTHER TWENTY-SEVEN YEARS.

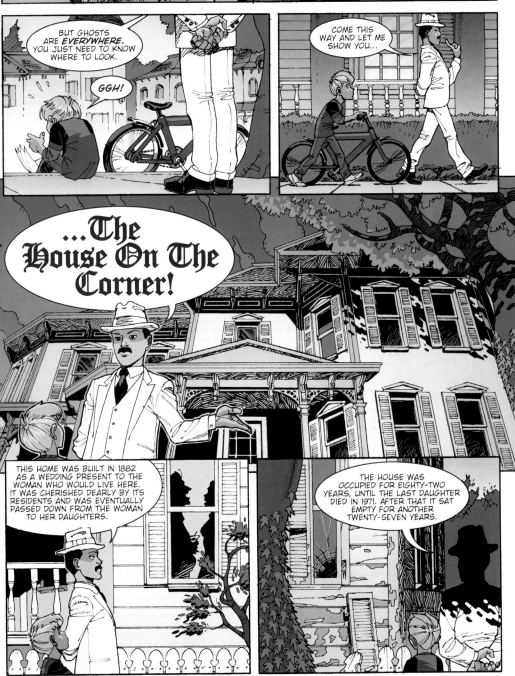

BY FREEWATER & MARANGON

"IN 1998 A RELATIVE OF THE PREVIOUS OWNER BOUGHT THE PROPERTY AND BEGAN TO RESTORE IT TO ITS ORIGINAL CONDITION.

"THE PARANORMAL EVENTS IN THE HOUSE STARTED OUT SLOWLY. THE NEW OWNER ENCOUNTERED ICY COLD SPOTS IN VARIOUS ROOMS. OFTEN, AFTER RAISING A WINDOW SHADE, HE WOULD RETURN ONLY TO FIND IT MYSTERIOUSLY LOWERED.

"AND, STRANGE AS IT MAY SEEM, THE CIRCUIT BOX HAD A HARD TIME STAYING IN THE *ON* POSITION."

UM... HELLO?

"WHEN THE NEW OWNER OF THE HOUSE FOUND A SANDER MOVED FROM ITS ORIGINAL RESTING PLACE TO THE CORNER OF THE ROOM, WITH ITS POWER CORD WRAPPED AROUND THE CLOSET DOOR, THE MEANING WAS UNCLEAR...

"...BUT THERE WAS NO MISTAKING THE INTENT OF WHAT THEY FOUND THE NEXT DAY.

"THIS OTHERWORLDLY MESSAGE WAS IGNORED, AND WORK ON THE HOUSE CONTINUED. AND SO DID THE HAUNTING."

♪

HEY!

POP!

"IF THE GHOST COULDN'T GET THE NEW OWNER TO LEAVE, THEN AT LEAST IT COULD COMMENT ON THE REDECORATING CHOICES..."

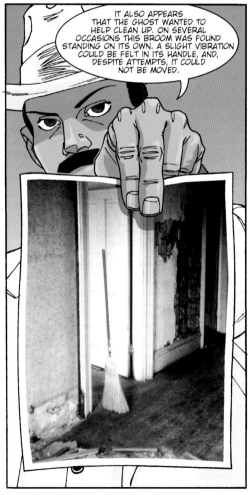

IT ALSO APPEARS THAT THE GHOST WANTED TO HELP CLEAN UP. ON SEVERAL OCCASIONS THIS BROOM WAS FOUND STANDING ON ITS OWN. A SLIGHT VIBRATION COULD BE FELT IN ITS HANDLE, AND, DESPITE ATTEMPTS, IT COULD NOT BE MOVED.

"OTHER THAN THE PHOTO OF THE BROOM, ATTEMPTS TO DOCUMENT THIS HAUNTING MET WITH FAILURE. IT WOULD SEEM THAT THE GHOST DIDN'T WANT OUTSIDERS TO KNOW WHAT WAS GOING ON.

"BUT OBVIOUSLY SHE HAD NO PROBLEM WITH SHOWING HERSELF TO HER NEW HOUSEMATES."

HEY... DO YOU SEE WHAT I SEE?

HUH?

WHAT IS IT? YOU SEE SOMETHING?

AN OLD WOMAN. SHE'S LOOKING RIGHT AT US...

THE WOMAN WAS LATER IDENTIFIED FROM PHOTO-GRAPHS AS THE LAST DAUGHTER OF THE ORIGINAL OWNER. SHE DIED IN 1971.

SOON AFTER, THE HAUNTINGS GREW FEWER AND FEWER, AS THE PREVIOUS OWNER GREW TO ACCEPT HER NEW HOUSE-MATES.

SO NEXT TIME YOU DOUBT THE EXISTENCE OF GHOSTS, JUST TAKE A CAREFUL LOOK AROUND.

LIKE I SAID... THEY'RE EVERYWHERE.

End

Spirit Rescue

An interview with séance medium
LARRY DRELLER

by SCOTT ALLIE

*A*fter failing out of college, Larry Dreller avoided the draft by joining the Navy. *After seeing a bit of the world, he returned to college, at the University of Denver, majoring in education and world history. He taught a variety of high-school subjects in the U.S., Canada, Australia, and England, before returning to Denver. There he taught briefly in Catholic schools, before settling into work with the state of Colorado, first in youth services, and later with the Department of Employment. Somehow all of this led to his current occupation, as a retiree heavily involved with the First Spiritual Science Church, where he conducts trainings and séances. He's written two books on his experiences and his gift, both for Weiser Books.*

ALLIE: Was Catholicism your religion of origin?

DRELLLER: No. I was brought up as a sort of hard-nosed Lutheran, and I converted to Roman Catholic because of my girlfriend. In those days you had to—I think you still do—and then she took off and became a nun. I really have some power there, don't I? But I just don't believe in organized religions. They're boring.

Even the Spiritualist church that you're part of now isn't actually the Spiritualist church—you said it was an off-branch?

It's an off-branch. The Spiritualists don't believe in reincarnation, and the church that I go to does, so they left the National Spiritualist church.

How did the Spiritualist church start?

It goes back roughly to 1848, with the Fox sisters. I believe the town was Hydesville, New York. Actually, there was some movement even before this. I can never remember his name, but there was a man about twenty-two years of age who had visions in New York. He coined a lot of phrases that eventually were taken over in the Spiritualist religion. But in 1848, Hydesville, New York, the Fox sisters heard noises in the basement, and found that they could communicate with the spirit. It was a traveling salesman named Charles Haynes, who was murdered and buried in the basement. This idea of contacting spirits became a sensation, which spread throughout the United States and into Europe. People threw in some Christianity and it became Spiritualism. Then came séances, table tipping, and eventually the Ouija board, which was very popular in the early 1900s. Spiritualism spread, and it really came to fruition around WWI when there was just a catastrophic loss of life. People wanted to find out if there is life after death. They didn't trust their organized religion.

I always thought the word Spiritualism referred to spirituality, but it's not merely spirituality as most people think of it, but—

Spirit communication. Life after death. The early Spiritualists started designing rituals, based on something called the power of the white light. The Spiritualists said the white light was sent from God, the universe, or Jesus, wherever. So you can see there's an intimate relationship between Christianity and Spiritualism. We have that ritual where we say that we believe in God, and we believe God is in everyone and everything, and God is love, and we are spiritual beings in a material existence. But mainly we create our own reality with our own thoughts. We also are very strong on the idea "question reality." Always question reality, because in our techno-materialist society, we're given a new reality, and we lose the reality and spirituality of ourselves.

In both books you talk a lot about different aspects of Zen discipline. Do distinctly Eastern traditions go all the way back to the origin of Spiritualism, or is that new?

That's a newer thing. A woman named Helen Blavatsky founded a movement called Theosophy, which helped bring Zen Buddhist meditation to the West. As with Spiritualists, Theosophists believe we go on to another place. In Buddhism, as you well know, we are reborn until we get rid of our negative karma. And that's in Spiritualism also.

Is that the Spiritualists' conflict with reincarnation—they believe we move beyond this life, rather than being reborn back into it?

Right—in Spiritualism, you go on to an astral plane, where you are learning the meaning of your previous life, and are now learning what the meaning of the universe is really about and how you fit into the scheme of things.

The first time you encountered a spirit, you were a teenager—is that right?

That was my grandfather, whom I never met in his life. He used to visit me in my dreams. A lot of the knowledge that you get from the spirit world does come through dreams. He told me to study harder and stop fighting my relatives. That there's more after this life. He taught me about spiritual baggage. You take all this stuff—who you are, your personality—with you. Do you want a negative personality, or do you want a positive personality? I told my grandmother about these dreams. She pulled out an old album, and there he was. And he was quite a dapper individual.

Then there was my grandmother's best friend who passed away. I went to her funeral and saw her. She was dressed up like a woman in the early fifties. The long gloves to the elbow, and a big picture hat. And she was young, and very, very pretty. Later I looked at the photos of her and she was a beauty, but not toward the end of her life.

From then on, my experiences really opened up. I think I had the gift very early. I supposedly suffered crib death twice. I can still remember the visions I saw as a baby—they stayed with me. To this day it scares the bejesus out of me. After you're in the craft for a long time, you know that life continues, but the thing is, when my time comes, I don't want to go. It's still mysterious. We're not given all the answers …

This is where the readership has to drop skeptical thoughts and realize that life does continue. The thing is, Scott, we are energy, we are essence. You remember the first law of thermodynamics? Everything in our universe is comprised of matter, which essentially means electromagnetic atoms, small jewels—everything that occupies space has energy. It can switch back and forth. I like to use the analogy of how water can be frozen—it changes form, and it can evaporate into steam. It can dissipate entirely, but it's energy. All the energy that has ever been created is still here. We change form. We're just quickly moving molecules which take on the appearance of solidity. So my hypothesis is that when we pass away our energy goes on.

And those experiences led you to Spiritualism?

Well, I was busy being a teenager, you know, raging, surging hormones. I didn't think as much about this stuff. Then I went into the Navy. It was in San Diego. We used to put a lot of the World War II ships and Korean war ships in mothballs—all sealed up. We'd salvage equipment from these old ships. Sextants never really get old—signal flags, binoculars. Even their jackets. One night I was on the night watch, and I vaguely heard this music. On a ship when the hatches are closed, you really can't hear anything.

Were you on the ship at this point?

I was on the ship. It was moored next to ours. I opened the hatches on the quartermaster locker. I opened it up, and there were three young sailors. One had red hair, and one was down on the floor playing cards. He had them spread out, and the other two were laughing. On the radio receivers— beautiful radios back then—there was this big-band music I later identified as Glenn Miller. I said, What are you guys doing here? They looked up at

69

me and disappeared. The cards stayed, and I put one in my pocket, and kept it for a long time. It was the queen of hearts.

It must have been a lot different than seeing the spirit of your grandfather in a dream, or seeing your grandmother's friend at a funeral. This must have been much more concrete.

Very, very personal. They weren't very far from me.

Was it scary for you, or were you getting accustomed to this sort of thing?

I was already used to having experiences. I could tell in high school whether a girl was going to turn me down. I could tell what the teacher was thinking. I did pretty well in school. You don't question it, because when you are a medium, or you're psychically aware, you have to be open and have a clear mind, and get rid of doubt.

Do you see a difference between a medium and a psychic?

Oh, they're really interrelated. A medium is a receiver between that higher world and this world. A séance medium contacts the departed, the deceased, or—ugly word—the dead! A psychic does things like readings, and has a precognitive skill. Sometimes they can have visions and so on, but they don't talk to the dead.

In the first book you talk about two kinds of mediums, referring to the particular methods the medium might use.

Right. The first is a mental medium, or trance medium, who uses his or her clairvoyant, clairaudient, or clairsentient gifts. Then you have your physical medium—or you did in the old days. They used to call them platform mediums, showbiz people. These are the ones that got into trouble with fraud. They had the ectoplasm—I saw a demonstration of that once, and I thought it was fascinating.

What was that like?

It's usually done in a soft light—red light is best, because it's an ethereal substance, as it's been explained to me. A deceased person gets into the physical medium's body, talks through their vocal chords, and then expels this ectoplasm. It comes out of the mouth and other body orifices. Sometimes it turns into little miniatures of the deceased person's head and face and arms, and so on. And talks. I've seen a demonstration where it came out of a person's mouth. It's not done much anymore because it was attacked by Harry Houdini and other people. But Sir Arthur Conan Doyle was very in awe of it. It's been reported that Queen Victoria held séances all the time.

When you were in the Navy, were you already starting to perform séances?

No. Oh, that came much later. It would be too strange in the Navy to go around and say, Let's have a séance.

How long ago was it that you started?

After the Navy I was a graduate student being tested by a graduate student in psychology. Someone from a long, long line of mediums trained me. His first name is Tim—I'll just let it be Tim. He came from generations of séance mediums in New Orleans, which seems to be America's most haunted place. We formed several study circles. We held a lot of séances, and talked to people.

You mentioned a ritual, but what does that consist of?

You should already know each other, you should have worked up to this for a little while before you really get into it, because some people have fear, some people are skeptical. You want to make sure that you're all singing from the same page. This is the way it was taught to me. We stand up, join hands, and then someone lights the candles, and convenes. We use white candles, lit with a wooden kitchen match. We bring these spirit forces into our bodies, asking for strength, protection, and guidance. They can make themselves known by odors, noise, temperature changes, and sighted appearances. When I've gotten really deeply into trance, I've called people in.

Is there a physical sensation that accompanies that?

There's a tingle. I have a tingling feeling; others have been flat, you know, nothing. You can't expect immediate results, but sometimes, boy, does it ever flow!

What happens when it is flowing? The whole group feels it?

Yes. Then we do the invocation—"The Spirits Above, the Spirits Below, the Spirits to the North of us, the Spirits to the South of us, the Spirits to the East of us, the Spirits to the West of us. Please attend us; answer our questions …" or do you have anything to say, or we would like to talk to you. It just all depends on what the group wants to accomplish.

Do you have a particular group that you work with?

I haven't been working with a group recently. I'm about to start some courses, and we're going over my second book now, doing corrections. There are several people here that are very gifted in astral projection, and have talked to spirits.

Beyond doing séances, you also purge unwanted spirits from homes.

I'm going to do one this weekend, as a matter of fact. It's simple. The Native Americans burned sage, cedar, and other natural plants, and I use that every so often. The Buddhists use incense, as do the Roman Catholics. The old

Spiritualists' way to purge starts with three cups of tap water and one cup of white vinegar—don't ask me why, it has to be white vinegar—and one cup of salt. I understand that sea salt works best. You bring it to boil in a pan, and you start from the bottom level of the building. All the windows, from bottom to top, must be open. You carry this steaming pan through each room.

That's basically a smudging.

Just like the Native Americans use. And in each room you ask that any spirit who is there leave this house in the holy white light and do not return. Go in peace. And that's a soul rescue.

So you're not so much chasing spirits out as helping them along?

Yes. When you want to get a spirit out of a haunting, you want to inform them that, yes, indeed, they're dead, and it's time to move on. It does no good to linger here.

What about unwanted spirits, or lower-level spirits? You say that these are the spirits of people who have kind of lived bad lives or who haven't—

Well, some of them are in paybacks. And you know, paybacks are a bitch. These malevolent spirits, or ghosts, are negative energy. That's the best way to put it. Scott, remember we talked about the revenants as well as the haunters? Revenants are people who have passed on, but are still sort of confused and have left behind vibrations and energy scars. There's a refusal to let go of who they were. They're confused and shocked, in a state of denial.

These are the angry ones. They don't want to go, or they had so much negative spiritual baggage, that they can't go. And they become haunters, which are angry, confused, and disbelieving spirits. They can become stronger and malevolent, feeding off the fear we project. They can linger around for centuries, because, remember, there is no concept of time.

Besides these sort of negative energies of humans who lived bad lives, do you encounter any other sort of spirits? Do you think there's such a thing as demons?

No, I think "demon" is a misused term. Demons are considered evil, but they weren't in ancient Greece—a demon was just a person that passed on—that's where the word comes from. Now we have the connotation that demons are evil, and ugly, and bad. I have, however, brushed shoulders several times with entities that I don't think had the best of intentions.

This is one thing that I haven't had enough personal experience with. The paranormal researchers have got to get in here and get it figured out. So far they've worked their way through ESP and precognition, but they have to really start investigating what these entities are.

So you think it's important to look at paranormal issues with the same kind of certainty that scientists look at their work?

Yes. But scientists are skeptics, because they rely on being able to weigh and classify, being able to see, touch, smell, hear—this type of thing. I never worry about skeptics. It will have to happen to them.

Scott, in the history of mankind, we have had hundreds of thousands to maybe millions of brushes with spirits. Is it all imagination? Come on. I know they exist. But how do you pull this out and let someone in a lab analyze it? The scientific community knows that something is amiss, and they are turning resources to it. They're looking at near death experiences, the whole light at the end of the tunnel we see. They say these experiences are due to medication, that the person isn't really dead, they had hypoxia, a lack of oxygen to the brain. And now they've come up with a new explanation, which I think is kind of cute—going through the tunnel and seeing the light is the brain revisiting the birth canal.

When we first spoke, I mentioned Hans Holzer, and you referred to him as the master—

He's the master.

He's no doubt the most famous ghost hunter in the twentieth century. But you're a lot more sympathetic to the spirits than Holzer. He was really chasing people—spirits—out of houses, in a much more old-fashioned way, treating spirits like pests. So I was a little surprised to hear you refer to him as the master, because it seems like what you do is very different. Also, he wasn't even a medium— he employed the services of others, like Sybil Leek, who also published a lot of books on her own adventures.

Well, Holzer is the intellectual scholar researcher. But let me ask you, how does he know so much? This man is obviously a medium, and just does not say that he is. He knows too much.

Why can't he just know from experience without actually having the sensitivity that you have?

I just feel from reading his books that he has brushed shoulders, or he wouldn't be in this area.

Well, he certainly brushed shoulders with a lot of entities. In his books he goes into great detail about the hauntings themselves. In a lot of instances, like the famous haunted hotel in San Diego, he didn't actually have the experiences—he relays the experiences of others, then brings in a medium to help him deal with it.

He just knows too much, and I think he has dabbled. That's why I feel he's the one who brought ghost investigation to the forefront. And in that, he is the master. There's a book that I would recommend very much. It's called, *Ghost: Investigating the Other Side*, by Katherine Ramsland. She's an investigative reporter. She was unconvinced in the first chapters, and in the end she knows it's so. Oh, I'm sure it has a lot to do with selling books, but I could tell from her tone that now she's a believer. The impartial, the distant, the skeptical—once they have one experience, it leads to the next, to the next, to the next.

Another big difference between you and Holzer is that your view of the entities is much more sympathetic. Holzer was a reflection of an older time, looking at ghosts simply as a problem. He'd just go in and get rid of them. What you do is more like therapy for the ghost, as well as therapy for the people there. You're very up-front that this approach to looking at the afterlife is a way for people to feel better about their present lives, to have a bigger picture about where their loved ones have gone, and maybe where they're going.

You hit it right on the head. We do have a survival of the personality, we take our essence with us, and you can call it a ghost, soul, spirit, energy, whatever. We let fear grow instead of trying to realize who these poor people were. But we can learn from them, which is what we do in the séances. I've been very lucky to be able to meet with one of my deceased relatives, my maternal grandmother, whom I loved very much, and to whom I dedicated my first book.

If a person believes that they are in a haunted house, that they're living with a spirit of some kind, what would your advice to them be?

If they feel they want to just get rid of it, they can then purge it with sea salt and vinegar. But I don't know if I'd want to call an exorcist. It's almost impossible—the Catholic Church looks the other way, and as Episcopalians go, it would really have to be proven. But if everything becomes really bad, deplorable and negative, move.

I thought you might say people shouldn't be scared, but you're saying it's natural to be afraid of these things.

Can you imagine, Scott, how many spirits, ghosts, essences, whatever, are with us right now? If we saw them all, we'd crack up.

My mother-in-law was living with us, my wife and children and me, and she said, You know that you're haunted here? She used to be kind of restless, an insomniac. She'd go downstairs to the family room and sleep on the couch. She said this man kept coming. He had red eyes, and was very, very tall. His head touched the ceiling. We had nine-foot-high ceilings, and he would stare at her. So she moved. After that, we were always visited at the same time, Wednesday evening about 9:00, by the smell of burned feathers or hair. Then it got very cold. The kids' clothes were always rearranged, thrown on the floor. Could have been a poltergeist. The kids were adolescent, and those teenage hormone surges are what they say brings on poltergeist activity. Anyway, this spirit would come and we'd smell this obnoxious odor. I had the electrician make sure there wasn't anything wrong, and it was at that particular time that we really got bombarded. It was warm, so there was no reason for the fireplaces in the neighborhood to be going. So it shouldn't be that odor of burning. But it would come through, and I thought, Well, let's get someone to deal with this. And that worked … at first. Then it came back a few months later, so I started doing my ritual, and it worked for a while, but it kept coming back.

Did you ever see the spirit that your mother-in-law referred to?

No, but neighborhoods in the suburbs being what they are, the neighborhood kids told us that there had been a suicide in our house—in my study, as a matter of fact. A teenage girl had tried to commit suicide several times. We sold the house and moved. Luckily it didn't come along with us. Sometimes they will—they'll follow you.

I've had a lot of interesting experiences, but I haven't put those in the books, because they'd just go on and on. And people want proof—although there are a heck of a lot of people that I run across who say, Hey, I loved your book—let me tell you about my experience!

When my wife and I actually did see some spirits was when we were newlyweds, and we were living in an apartment in Capitol Hill, here in Denver. It's an older neighborhood, and we were visited several times by a young man standing at the foot of our bed. My wife finally saw it, so she became sort of a believer. And we moved. We found out from the landlord that the man had committed suicide in our place. Thanks for telling us! You know, because I would not have moved in! I'd thought the deal was awfully good. I didn't use any of my arts to get rid of him, I just said to Lana, my wife, Let's move!

Then two years ago we went to New Orleans, and we were staying with these friends in one of their timeshares, in one of the oldest sections of New Orleans. There was a hospital there dating back to the French. We were staying with this couple—in separate rooms, Scott. Anyway, the gal we were staying with—she's very scientific, very rational—she said, Boy, I feel uneasy here! And even her husband said, I just feel creepy and crawly. And they didn't sleep at all. Then one night there was a raging storm in New Orleans—you know what it's like down there when they get thunder and lightning? Well, the lightning lit up the window, and there was this young soldier in a strange outfit, very Battle of New Orleans—

A Civil War uniform?

Civil War or something like that. I vaguely recognized his bandolier and his hat, as he was standing at the end of the bed. We were in New Orleans for about five, six days, and he stayed there. He'd stare down at me, and it gave me the creeps. Poor kid. He wasn't more than sixteen or seventeen years of age. Well, anyway, I was talking to a lady down on the wharf—she was running a tourist booth, and she said, Where are you staying? And I told her, and she got big eyes and looked at me, and she said, Oh my God! She used to own that place, but she left it because the ghosts kept bothering her kids. One night she'd been washing the dishes, and the dishes started flying around, smashing against things. And she said it was time to get out of there.

We also went to several of the plantations—Oh, my God, the vibrations were so incredible. I got headaches, and I'd have to get out of the tour and go outside. I'd hear banjo music in one place. My hair was being touched—what little hair I have left was being stroked, and I could feel cobwebs over my face, breath blowing in my ears. I always get nervous, Scott, because I don't want them to come with me. I'm afraid they're going to piggyback on me. I kept thinking of white light, white light, white light. A misty white light surrounding me.

Scott, I've had so many wonderful things, been gifted with so many wonderful encounters. There comes a point, when you're at a cocktail party or something—I start talking about it, and you should see their eyes. I just say, Oh ho ho, just kidding. And I move on, because it's not fully acceptable. But when science devotes itself to investigating hauntings, my God, they get these wonderful sightings, some of which show up on the real high-speed film. I have a friend that is doing that. He's a commercial photographer, but he's going after spirits now. When they get these photographs, people say, Oh, it's been doctored! Or it's the light coming in through the drapes—we have a million excuses for why it can happen. Scott, think about when it becomes provable—we have a place to go to when we die. What a neat thing! Our personality does survive. It's not the end.

Larry Dreller is a practicing medium, and has been for several decades. His books on these experiences, Beginner's Guide to Mediumship *and the upcoming* Secrets of a Medium, *are available from better bookstores, or the publisher, Weiser Books (800/423-7087).*

IT WAS THE SUMMER THAT I WAS ELEVEN.

OR MAYBE WHEN I WAS TWELVE. YOU'D THINK I'D REMEMBER THE DETAILS -- CONSIDERING WHAT HAPPENED LATER -- BUT. . .

. . .WELL, I DON'T WANT TO GET AHEAD OF MYSELF.

SO, IT WAS THE SUMMER OF EITHER 1967, OR '68. I'D RIDDEN MY BIKE THE SWEATY FOUR MILES FROM HOME, UP THE BACKSIDE OF JORGENSEN'S HILL, TO OUR "HIDEOUT."

I WAS ALONE. MY FRIEND DENNIS WAS STILL RECOVERING FROM THE NASTY SPILL HE'D TAKEN RIDING WITH HIS BROTHER DOWN THE OTHER SIDE OF THE HILL.

A LESSON: DON'T RIDE TWO-ON-A-BIKE DOWN A MILE-LONG HILL ON A PAVED ROAD THAT TURNS INTO LOOSE GRAVEL AT THE BOTTOM.

LIES, DEATH, AND OLFACTORY DELUSIONS

WRITTEN BY RANDY STRADLEY   ART BY PAUL CHADWICK   COLORS AND LETTERS BY MICHELLE MADSEN

I HID MY BIKE UNDER THE BRIDGE. NOBODY KNEW ABOUT OUR SECRET PLACE, AND WE MEANT TO KEEP IT THAT WAY.

OF COURSE, A FEW YEARS LATER, I BROUGHT A GIRLFRIEND THERE FOR AN ABORTIVE MAKE-OUT SESSION. SHE NEVER FORGAVE ME FOR NOT WARNING HER ABOUT THE GOOEY STRANDS OF TAR HANGING UNDERNEATH THE BRIDGE. AND WE NEVER ACTUALLY MADE IT TO THE HIDEOUT. . .

GETTING IN WAS ALWAYS A PAIN -- LITERALLY. WE LOST COUNT OF THE NUMBER OF BLACKBERRY THORNS WE PULLED OUT OF OUR HANDS AND KNEES.

BUT WE FIGURED THE DISCOMFORT WAS THE PRICE WE PAID TO KEEP LESS ADVENTURESOME SNOOPS OUT.

THE ENTRANCE HAD PROBABLY BEEN MADE BY THE COMINGS AND GOINGS OF A RACCOON.

WE WIDENED IT -- BUT ONLY A LITTLE . . .

OW.

THE REAL EXCAVATION WAS FURTHER IN.

THIS WAS OUR SPOT.

NOT MUCH GOOD IN BAD WEATHER -- THE RAIN CAME STRAIGHT THROUGH -- BUT IT WAS GREAT IN THE SUMMER.

I HAD NO REAL OBJECTIVE IN COMING TO THE HIDEOUT THAT DAY.

I HAD READ EVERY COMIC BOOK AND LOOKED AT EVERY PLAYBOY THAT WE HAD STASHED THERE UNTIL THEY WERE COMMITTED TO MEMORY.

I GUESS I JUST WANTED TO GET AWAY FROM MY SISTER AND HER FRIENDS.

"I'M 'DAPPLED,'" I REMEMBER THINKING.

AND THEN I NOTICED SOMETHING ELSE.

SNIFF SNIFF

I KNEW EXACTLY WHAT IT WAS.

I HAD SMELLED THAT SMELL OFTEN ENOUGH . . .

. . . BUT HE COULDN'T HAVE FOUND THIS PLACE. COULD HE?

LARRY?

HI.
GAH!
ER'S GENERAL STORE
Coca-Co
FUNNY. AS SCARED AS I'D BEEN TEN MINUTES EARLIER, I STILL STOPPED AT TROTTER'S GENERAL STORE FOR A GRAPE SODA . . . JUST LIKE ALWAYS.
MAYBE WHEN YOU'RE A KID YOU DON'T KNOW ENOUGH TO **KNOW** THAT STUFF LIKE THAT ISN'T SUPPOSED TO HAPPEN, SO YOU LET IT GO SOONER THAN YOU WOULD OTHERWISE. SURE, IT WAS WEIRD. AND SCARY. BUT I NEVER MENTIONED IT. TO ANYBODY.
ICE
BESIDES, IT WAS **EASTLING**.

NOBODY IN OUR CLASS LIKED EASTLING.

EVERYBODY MAKE SURE YOU HAVE A SHARP PENCIL. I DON'T WANT ANY INTERRUPTIONS DURING THE TEST.

I'M GONNA MAKE MY PENCIL REALLY SHARP!

LARRY WAS ONE OF THOSE KIDS WHO WASN'T FRIENDS WITH *ANYBODY* -- THOUGH HE TRIED TO BE FRIENDS WITH *EVERYBODY*.

WORSE, HE *SMELLED.* BAD.

WHETHER IT WAS PURELY A QUESTION OF HYGIENE, OR IF HE SUFFERED FROM SOME ILLNESS OR OTHER UNAVOIDABLE SOURCE OF ODOR, I NEVER FOUND OUT.

NOT THAT IT WOULD HAVE MATTERED TO ANYBODY...

IS SOMETHIN' WRONG?

I *ASKED* IF SOMETHING IS WRONG.

YOU LOOK LIKE YOU CAN'T *BREATHE.*

NO. I'M ALL RIGHT.

THE HELL I WAS.

JUST A WHIFF OF LARRY COULD SINGE YOUR NOSE HAIRS.

HA! YOUR EYES ARE WATERING!

≈GASP≈ SHUT UP, DENNIS.

I NEVER WENT OUT OF MY WAY TO BE MEAN TO LARRY, THE WAY SOME OF THE OTHERS DID.

I'D SPENT A FEW YEARS AS THE CLASS "MISFIT" MYSELF.

THAT COULD BE WHY HE ALWAYS TRIED HARDEST TO BE *MY* FRIEND.

MAYBE THAT'S WHY *I'M* TELLING THIS STORY...

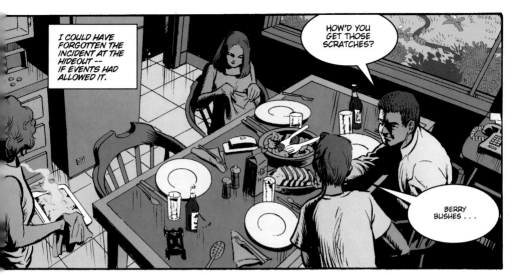

I COULD HAVE FORGOTTEN THE INCIDENT AT THE HIDEOUT -- IF EVENTS HAD ALLOWED IT.

HOW'D YOU GET THOSE SCRATCHES?

BERRY BUSHES . . .

HOW WERE THINGS HERE, TODAY?

I GOT A CALL FROM VELMA ZIGLER AT THE WOMEN'S CLUB --

THERE WAS AN ACCIDENT ON RAINBOW LANE YESTERDAY.

A BOY WAS KILLED...

DENNIS LIVED ON RAINBOW LANE.

HE WAS ABOUT YOUR AGE, BUT I DON'T KNOW IF HE WAS IN YOUR CLASS. . .

RELIEF. IT WASN'T DENNIS.

. . . DO YOU -- DID YOU -- KNOW LARRY EASTLING?

ISN'T HE THE ONE WHO STINKS?

VELMA SAID SOME OTHER KIDS CHASED HIM ONTO THE ROAD AND HE WAS HIT BY ONE OF THE TRUCKS FROM THE TILE FACTORY. . .

THAT EVENING SEEMED TO LAST FOREVER, BUT ALL I REMEMBER OF IT WAS A DULL ROAR IN MY EARS AND A COLD WEIGHT IN MY GUT.

81

LATER, I FOUND MOM DIGGING AROUND IN MY CLOSET.

WHAT'RE YOU LOOKING FOR?

MRS. ZIGLER SAYS THE EASTLING FAMILY DOESN'T HAVE MUCH MONEY.

YOU'VE OUTGROWN YOUR SUNDAY SUIT --

-- SO I'M DONATING IT TO THE EASTLINGS SO THEY CAN HAVE LARRY *BURIED* IN IT.

THOUGHTS OF LARRY AND DEATH STAYED WITH ME FOR THE NEXT FEW DAYS. THAT, AND *SOMETHING ELSE.*

I'D NEVER KNOWN ANYBODY WHO'D DIED BEFORE.

THE DIFFERENCE BETWEEN MORTALITY AS A CONCEPT AND AS A *REALITY* PUT MY BRAIN INTO OVERDRIVE.

I RELIVED EVERY CRUELTY TOWARD LARRY -- NO MATTER HOW MINOR -- THAT I HAD EVER INSTIGATED, OR PARTICIPATED IN.

I TRIED TO MITIGATE AND RATIONALIZE MY ACTIONS, BUT I COULDN'T LIE TO MYSELF. . .

. . . I HAD BEEN AWARE OF LARRY'S LONELINESS AND HURT -- HAVING LIVED THROUGH A DEGREE OF THE SAME TREATMENT MYSELF.

I WAS GUILTY, AND LARRY WAS DEAD.

I WONDERED ABOUT LARRY.

I WONDERED IF DEATH HURT.

I MEAN, I WAS PRETTY SURE THAT BEING HIT BY A TRUCK HURT . . .

. . . BUT WHAT DID BEING DEAD FEEL LIKE?

I ASKED MY DAD ABOUT IT. HE SAID YOU DIDN'T FEEL ANYTHING -- YOU WERE DEAD.

MOM SAID YOU FELT FINE -- IF YOU WENT TO HEAVEN.

DENNIS AND I HAD THE INEVITABLE DISCUSSION: WHAT IF YOU WERE DEAD, BUT AWARE OF EVERYTHING THAT WAS HAPPENING TO YOUR BODY? HE SAID YOU'D FEEL IT IN YOUR TOES FIRST, BECAUSE THEY BURIED YOU BAREFOOT.

I DIDN'T MENTION THE OTHER THING TO ANYBODY. . .

. . . BUT THE SMELL WAS REALLY GETTING TO ME.

IT WAS LARRY, NO DOUBT ABOUT IT.

NO ONE ELSE IN THE HOUSE NOTICED.

YET HIS ESSENCE FILLED MY ROOM.

I KNEW WHERE IT WAS COMING FROM.

BY THE FIFTH NIGHT, I COULDN'T IGNORE IT ANY LONGER.

GASP
LARRY. . . ?
Y-YOU'RE DEAD. . .
YEAH . . . I GUESS.
BUT I DON'T SMELL BAD ANYMORE . . .
. . . DO I?
N-NO . . . NOT ANYMORE . . .
THANKFULLY, I NEVER SAW -- OR SMELLED -- LARRY AGAIN.
I GUESS THAT EVEN THE SMALLEST GESTURE OF ACCEPTANCE MADE HIS DEPARTURE -- TO WHERE EVER HE WAS GOING -- EASIER FOR HIM.
I HAD DENIED HIM IN LIFE, YET HE STILL SOUGHT ME OUT.
I JUST HOPE LARRY NEVER FINDS OUT THAT I LIED TO HIM IN DEATH . . .
END

No one remembers how many nights the summoning took.
AAAOOOOOOOOO
OOOOOAAAHWOO
Some say as many as five, while others insist he arrived after the very first appeal.
This is understandable, given the fact that dogs aren't exactly known for their keen sense of time.
AH, THIS IS NUTS! I'M TIRED OF BARKIN' MY THROAT DRY NIGHT AFTER NIGHT FOR NOTHIN'.
MAYBE WE'RE DOING IT WRONG.
OH NO! MY GRANDPA TOLD ME WHEN I WAS A PUP... "HOWL AT MIDNIGHT, THREE STRONG."
then again, they did put grandpa down the next day.
IF YOU ASK ME, YOU'RE ALL PRIZE CHUMPS. WHOEVER HEARD OF A WISE DOG ANY-WAY? I MEAN, YOU SLOBS LICK YOUR OWN...
STIFLE IT CAT, 'LESS YOU WANT TO LOSE A FEW LIVES.
SNIF, SNIF!
HEY! GUYS-- LOOK!
I HEARD YOUR CALL.
WHAT IS YOUR TROUBLE?

STRAY - by EVAN DORKIN & JILL THOMPSON

W-WELL, SIR, IT'S OUR FRIEND, JACK.
HE--WELL, IT'S AWFUL HARD TO DESCRIBE--
HE'S CRAZY! SAYS THERE'S A DEAD DOG LIVIN' IN HIS YARD!
PUGSLEY!
HMM.
WHERE CAN I FIND HIM?
HIS YARD'S RIGHT OVER HERE! FOLLOW ME!
HIT THE BRICKS, RAT BREATH. THIS IS CANINE BUSINESS.
AW, GO CHASE AN ONCOMING CAR!
THANK YOU FOR COMING, SIR.
WE ARE HONORED BY YOUR PRESENCE.
THIS IS MY FRIEND, JACK.
HE DESPERATELY NEEDS YOUR HELP.
HMM. SO JACK, WHAT CAN I DO FOR YOU?
WELL, YOU SEE SIR... MY FAMILY MOVED HERE JUST THIS SUMMER.
AND THEY BUILT ME A HOUSE. A REALLY WONDERFUL HOUSE, ACTUALLY.
BUT, I HAVEN'T BEEN ABLE TO SLEEP ONE FULL NIGHT IN IT.
BECAUSE IT'S HAUNTED.
JACK

Sniff Snif! Go on. I'm listening.
Well, uh, first it got cold. Really, really cold, even on warm nights.
Then I started smelling things, hearing things like a dog crying.
Aw, the house was probably just settling.
Can it, Pugs.
"At first I thought I was having a nightmare--or that I ate some bad food. But every night it was the same.
WWOOOOOO
I heard the cries too, from next door...
It was awful.
Ah, you're both eatin' outta the same bowl. I been walked around the block a few times an' I never heard nothin' crazy like that.'
"Neither did my masters. They just thought I was sick. Three vets couldn't find anything wrong with me. The stupid pet psychic found plenty, though..."
Jack's telling me he needs more affection. More attention.
I am not! I just want a decent night's sleep!
People! Please don't listen to this moron!
But the sounds didn't stop. They just got worse. I've been afraid to sleep in my house, even in the rain!
He was in terrible shape, sir. That's when I called a meeting. And we decided to call for help.
Yes, well it is possible that some great unhappiness took place here. I do sense a cold spot, which often indicates a restless spirit.

Y-Y-YOU MEAN A GHOST? A F-FOR REAL DEAD GHOST?
DO YOU ALL GOT WORMS? GHOSTS AIN'T REAL! THEM'S JUST STORIES. STUFF THEY TELL YOU AT THE PUPPY FARM TO KEEP YOU FROM RUNNIN' AROUND AT NIGHT.
YEAH, WELL, REAL OR NOT, IF I SEE SOME OLD GHOST, I'LL BITE IT. I'M NOT AFRAID!
WE MUST DIG OUT THE COLD SPOT. THE PROBLEM LIES BENEATH THE HOUSE. I AM SURE OF IT.
UH, MY OWNERS WON'T LIKE THIS. THEY'RE VERY PARTICULAR ABOUT THEIR YARD.
I COULD KILL A MOLE OR RACCOON AND THROW IT IN THE HOLE.
YOU'D LOOK LIKE A HERO.
UM, NO. THAT'S OKAY.
DON'T WORRY, BOY, ALL WILL BE WELL SOON.
RABIES. IT'S GOTTA BE! YOU'RE ALL NUTS.
And so they dug deep down into the cold earth for what seemed like hours. and just when it seemed they could dig no further...
the earth gave up one of its secrets.
WHITEY, WOULD YOU PLEASE STOP SNIFFING MY ASS? I'M WORKIN' HERE!
oh. uh sorry, ace... nervous habit.
WHOA. HOLD UP. I SEE SOMETHIN'.

WOW! BONES! LOTS OF BONES! OH BOY OH BOY OH BOY!
QUIT DROOLIN', YOU DUMB AMINAL. THOSE ARE DOG BONES.
ooooh. ick.
THERE'S A COLLAR, TOO! MIGHT HAVE SOME I.D.
SNIF.
OLD. MAYBE FIFTY YEARS.
HER NAME WAS... TRIXIE.
SAY, DID IT JUST GET COLDER?
WHAT THE--?!
EEE-YIPE!
REX! WAIT!
THAT PUNK. HE RAN LIKE A DAMN SQUIRREL.
HELL, EVEN WHITEY STOOD HIS GROUND. SURE, HE PISSED HIMSELF. BUT HE STAYED FIRM.
HMM. WE'LL NEED TO PERFORM A SUMMONING TO RELEASE THE SPIRIT. AND WITH THE DOBERMAN GONE WE'LL NEED ONE MORE SET OF PAWS TO COMPLETE THE CIRCLE.

HOW MUCH LONGER DO WE HAVE TO SIT HERE? MY TAIL FELL ASLEEP AN HOUR AGO!
DIDN'T YOU HEAR? HE SAID KEEP STILL, CAT.
IT'S ALL RIGHT. THE RITUAL ISN'T WORKING. HER SPIRIT SHOULD HAVE BEEN COAXED OUT BY NOW.
SOMETIMES THEY NEED A GOOD JOLT. SOMETHING TO SHAKE THEM LOOSE, YOU MIGHT SAY.
YEAH? WHAT KIND OF JOLT?
THIS KIND.
WHOA! HEY! HEY, FTT! FTT!
...
AW, ME AN' MY STUPID CURIOSITY.
OW.
GRRRRUF RUF!! ROWF ROWF ROWFF

IT'S ALL RIGHT, TRIXIE.
YOU'RE AMONG FRIENDS HERE.
WE WANT TO HELP.
CAN YOU REMEMBER HOW YOU GOT HERE?
I... came such a long way...
My family was moving cross-country, but I got lost chasing a cat. I found my way back but they were gone.
For months I trailed their faint scent.
Finally, just when I was about to give up, I tracked them to this neighborhood.
I ran the last few yards to the house, but in my excitement I failed to notice **the car.**
The driver read my tags, reeking of beer. Afraid that he'd **killed his new neighbor's dog** he **panicked** and buried me in his yard.
But I wasn't dead, yet. I awoke in the dark, where I've been all these years...
...waiting for someone to answer my cry for help. Thank you, all of you. Now I'm free to rejoin my family at last. It won't be hard to find them this time...

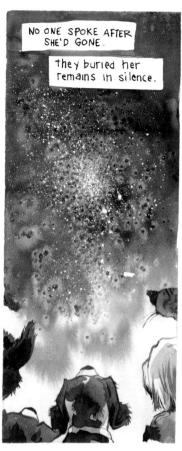

NO ONE SPOKE AFTER SHE'D GONE.

they buried her remains in silence.

YOU'LL HAVE NO MORE TROUBLES NOW. THIS DOG-HOUSE IS **CLEAN**.

I THINK WE'D ALL BEST GO HOME, NOW, BEFORE THIS STORM GETS WORSE.

YES, SIR. AND **THANK** YOU, SIR.

They padded off to their homes and hideaways, wondering if it had all been a dream.

Wondering what it would be like when the black dog came to claim them.

But Jack could only think of sleep.

ALL RIGHT, COME ON.

And how wonderful it was to have his house back.

THE END

Our Artists and Writers

A graduate of the University of Cincinnati with a degree in painting, **PHILIP CRAIG RUSSELL** has run the gamut in comics. After establishing a name for himself at Marvel, he went on to become one of the pioneers in opening new vistas for this underestimated field. He has created award-winning adaptations of operas such as Wagner's *The Ring of the Nibelung* and Mozart's *The Magic Flute*, as well as his ongoing project, retelling the fairy tales of Oscar Wilde. He has become a highly respected artist's artist with his fine-lined, realistic style, and revolutionary storytelling.

MIKE RICHARDSON is the publisher of Dark Horse Comics and the president of Dark Horse Entertainment, for which he has produced numerous projects for film and television. Co-author of *Comics Between the Panels* and *Blast Off!*, Mike is an enthusiastic collector of vintage toys and comics. Mike and his wife, Karie, live with their three daughters in Lake Oswego, Oregon.

MIKE MIGNOLA is the award-winning creator of the comic-book *Hellboy*, and spent part of this year working on the film version with director Guillermo del Toro. Mignola's other comics work includes best-selling books for both Marvel and DC Comics, as well as work for almost every other major publisher. In Hollywood he has worked as an artist and designer with Francis Ford Coppola and Disney on the films *Dracula* and *Atlantis*, respectively. He lives in Manhattan with his wife and daughter.

GARY GIANNI graduated from The Chicago Academy of Fine Arts in 1976. His artwork has appeared in *The Chicago Tribune*, numerous magazines, children's books, and paperbacks. Gianni debuted his work in the comics field in 1990 and has since been recognized with the Eisner Award for Best Short Story. He is perhaps best known for his ink drawing and oil paintings for a number of book collections, including *The Savage Tales of Solomon Kane*.

British writer and news correspondent **PERCEVAL LANDON** (1869-1927), in addition to writing "Thurnley Abbey" and other gothic stories, visited and wrote books on such countries as Tibet, Lhasa, and Nepal, and edited John Parmenter's horticultural book *Heliotropes, or New Posies for Sundials*.

PAUL LEE is a painter and freelance illustrator, the creator of the comics series *Lurid*, and co-creator of *The Devil's Footprints*. He has worked closely with Brian Horton, most notably on Dark Horse's *Buffy the Vampire Slayer* covers. He recommends fiber to promote regularity, and lives with his wife and son in Southern California.

BRIAN HORTON has been an illustrator and video-game artist for ten years. He's worked for interactive companies including Disney, Dreamworks, and Electronic Arts. At EA he was the Lead Artist on *Clive Barker's Undying*, and for the past two years has been at The Collective, art directing *Indiana Jones and the Emperor's Tomb*. Brian moonlights in comics with his partners in crime, Scott Allie and Paul Lee, on *Buffy*, *Star Wars*, and *The Devil's Footprints*. He shares his life with his wife Susan and son Victor in Aliso Viejo, California.

SCOTT ALLIE writes and edits comics and stories for Dark Horse Comics and other publishers. He lives in Portland, Oregon with his wife Melinda and their phantom cat, Shadow.

After growing up in Munich, Germany, **ULI OESTERLE** suffered a bout of acoustic aphasia (a brain malady which impairs the ability to understand language) for a month in the early nineties. His comics stories have since centered on frenzy and broken lunatics. His first full-length comic, *Brain Songs*, was published in Germany in 1999, and later translated into English. He lives with his girlfriend Daniela and young son Vincent, and is at work on his series *Hector Umbra*, about a man who can see other people's delusions.

Born in Santa Fe, Argentina in 1971, **LUCAS MARANGON** attended the Manuel Belgrano School of Graphic Design and Advertising, and soon got work as a professional illustrator. In 1995 he moved to Mexico City and began his work as a comic-book artist. Lucas continues to draw comics for Dark Horse, including the series *R.I.P.D.* and short stories in *Star Wars Tales*.

MILTON FREEWATER, JR. died in a tragic accident in 1997 during a trip to Walla Walla, when, deciding to spend the night in his car, he unwittingly parked directly on top of train tracks. He's the only real ghost writing for this anthology. But don't tell him, because he does not know he's dead.

PAUL CHADWICK, descendant of Oregon Governor Stephen Chadwick and of President John Tyler, found their portraits spooky growing up. He later realized their expressions were accusatory, given the degeneration of the family indicated by his chosen profession. A cartoonist since 1984, he's best known for the brain-transplant-victim saga *Concrete*, and less so for *The World Below*, a melange of Lovecraft, Freud, and Kirby.

RANDY STRADLEY has been writing comics now for twenty years, and editing them for almost as many. It is perhaps for that reason that his memories of growing up in a small town in rural Oregon are so foggy that he now believes that the events in his story in this book might actually be true.

JILL THOMPSON is a renowned illustrator and the creator of the award-winning, all-ages cartoon-book series *Scary Godmother*. Her work has been seen in books ranging from *Classics Illustrated* and *Wonder Woman* to *Sandman*. Jill is a longtime resident of Chicago, where she lives with her husband, the comic-book writer Brian Azzarello.

EVAN DORKIN is the Harvey, Eisner, and Ignatz Award-winning creator of *Milk and Cheese* and *Dork* from Slave Labor Graphics, and various Marvel, Dark Horse, and DC comics. His cartooning has appeared in *Esquire*, *Spin*, *The Onion*, *Disney Adventures*, and *Nickelodeon* magazine. With Sarah Dyer, he's written for *Space Ghost Coast to Coast*, *Superman*, and *Batman Beyond*, and was creator, writer, and executive producer of *Welcome to Eltingville*, his very own failed pilot that aired on the Cartoon Network throughout 2002.

More adventure, terror, and laughs from Dark Horse Comics

Mike Mignola's Hellboy

Seed of Destruction
trade paperback
ISBN:1-56971-316-2 $17.95

Wake the Devil
trade paperback
ISBN:1-56971-226-3 $17.95

The Chained Coffin & Others
trade paperback
ISBN:1-56971-349-9 $17.95

The Right Hand of Doom
trade paperback
ISBN:1-56971-489-4 $17.95

Conqueror Worm
trade paperback
ISBN:1-56971-699-4 $17.95

The Art of Hellboy
large format hardcover
ISBN:1-56971-910-1 $49.95

BPRD: Hollow Earth
trade paperback
ISBN:1-56971-862-8 $17.95

Hellboy:Weird Tales Volume 1
trade paperback
ISBN:1-56971-622-6 $17.95

Paul Chadwick's Concrete

Fragile Creature
trade paperback
ISBN:1-56971-022-8 $15.95

Killer Smile
trade paperback
ISBN: 1-56971-080-5 $16.95

The Complete Concrete
trade paperback
ISBN:1-56971-037-6 $24.95

P. Craig Russell

The Ring of the Nibelung
Volume 1
trade paperback
ISBN:1-56971-666-8 $21.95

Volume 2
trade paperback
ISBN:1-56971-734-6 $21.95

Murder Mysteries
written by Neil Gaiman
hardcover
ISBN:1-56971-634-X $13.95

Isolation and Illusion
trade paperback
ISBN:1-56971-916-0 $14.95

The Devil's Footprints
Scott Allie, Paul Lee & Brian Horton
trade paperback
ISBN:1-56971-933-0 $14.95

The Goon Volume 1: Nothin' But Misery
Eric Powell
trade paperback
ISBN:1-56971-998-5 $15.95

Scatterbrain
featuring Mike Mignola, Evan Dorkin
& others
large format hardcover
ISBN:1-56971-426-6 $19.95

AVAILABLE AT YOUR LOCAL COMICS SHOP OR BOOKSTORE
To find a comics shop in your area,
call 1-888-266-4226

For more information or to order
direct visit darkhorse.com or call
1-800-862-0052
Mon.-Sat. 9 A.M. to 5 P.M.
Pacific Time

*Prices and availability subject
to change without notice

DARK HORSE COMICS™